Step-by-Step

OUTDOOR WOODWORK

Step-by-Step
OUTDOOR
WOODWORK

Over twenty easy-to-build projects for your patio and garden

Mike Lawrence

NEW HOLLAND

First published in the UK in 1993 by
New Holland (Publishers) Ltd
Chapel House, 24 Nutford Place
London W1H 6DQ

Reprinted 1994 and 1995

ISBN 1 85368 230 6 (hbk)
ISBN 1 85368 225 X (pbk)

Co-ordination and picture research: Elizabeth Whiting & Associates
Editor: Dek Messecar
US consultant: Derek Bradford AIA RIBA
Design: Cooper Wilson Design
Illustration: Rob Shone
Originated by Scantrans (Pte) Ltd
Printed and bound by Times Offset (M) Sdn. Bhd.

The author would especially like to thank the following for their invaluable assis-
tance: Armatool Distributors Ltd., Black & Decker, Clifton Nurseries, Lloyd Christie
Garden Architects and Stanley Tools for loan of tools for special photography.
Design of aviary: Anne Kelly
Special project design: D.K.M. Design

Contents

INTRODUCTION

IF YOU WANT TO TURN YOUR GARDEN FROM A FLAT PLOT OF LAND INTO A LANDSCAPE WITH SOME PHYSICAL FEATURES, WOOD IS THE OBVIOUS CHOICE OF BUILDING MATERIAL FOR EVERYTHING FROM FENCES TO SUMMERHOUSES. BECAUSE WOOD IS SUCH A VERSATILE MATERIAL, THERE IS VIRTUALLY NO LIMIT TO WHAT YOU CAN DO WITH IT. THE ONLY POSSIBLE RESTRICTION WILL BE YOUR OWN LEVEL OF WOODWORKING SKILLS, BUT EVEN AMATEUR CARPENTERS WITH TEN THUMBS CAN BUILD PERFECTLY ACCEPTABLE STRUCTURES OUT OF DOORS WHERE THE EYE IS LESS CRITICAL OF SLIGHTLY OUT-OF-SQUARE JOINTS OR A LESS-THAN-IMMACULATE FINISH ON WHATEVER YOU DECIDE TO TURN YOUR HAND TO.

In the various sections of this book you will find woodworking projects ranging from the simplest, such as a bird table or a window box, to more complex structures. The section on fences and gates deals with all the most commonly used types, and tells you everything you need to know about choosing and erecting them, plus tips on keeping them in good working order.

Next, you will find details about building pergolas and walkways in a range of styles and materials over which you can train your climbing plants, plus how to use trellis to best advantage.

Your garden is sure to need paths and steps, plus somewhere to sit out when the lawn is wet or soft, so the next section starts with using wood for natural-looking path and step surfaces, then covers building timber decks and goes on to deal with erecting gazebos and summerhouses that will enable you to form the perfect centrepiece for your garden design.

While you are busy relaxing, children expect to be entertained, and the next section on play equipment covers everything a child could want, from swings, seesaws and slides to sand pits, climbing frames and tree houses. There is even a design for a colourful and highly unusual garden aviary.

Finally, there is a selection of small weekend projects for you to tackle, followed by a comprehensive reference section that covers the tools and materials you will need to use and the basic techniques you will be employing repeatedly as you work.

Throughout, there are colour photographs and detailed illustrations to show how everything is put together. The accompanying text and captions take you through every stage of each project from estimating and buying materials to constructing and finishing whatever you have chosen to make. It even encourages you to try out variations on the themes illustrated, to help you create a range of garden features and structures that will be uniquely your own creation.

Follow our instructions, and you will be able to fence your garden, furnish it, create features that will enhance the view, encourage plants to grow, and even provide a sheltered retreat where you can escape the pressures of everyday life for a while and commune quietly with nature!

Above: *Even the simplest structures such as a rustic pergola and a timber seat can provide a focal point in the garden.*

Left: *Timber is the perfect material for the more formal features of your property, such as boundary fences and gates.*

Right: *Every garden needs somewhere cool and shady, and a trellised arbour is a stylish and practical way of providing it.*

Below: *A tree house is every child's idea of the perfect hiding place, and is easy to construct from scrap timber.*

FENCES

FENCES ARE THE MOST POPULAR BOUNDARY MARKERS AROUND. THEY ARE WIDELY AVAILABLE, COME IN A RANGE OF TYPES, ARE EASY TO PUT UP AND MAINTAIN, AND NEED NOT COST THE EARTH. OF THE MAIN ALTERNATIVES, WALLS ARE OF COURSE MORE DURABLE, BUT TAKE TIME AND EFFORT TO BUILD AND WILL COST A GREAT DEAL MORE THAN A FENCE, WHILE HEDGES ARE FINE IF YOU CAN AFFORD TO WAIT FOR THEM TO GROW AND ARE PREPARED TO LOOK AFTER THEM REGULARLY TO ENSURE THAT THEY REMAIN FIT AND HEALTHY. BUT IF MONEY AND TIME ARE BOTH IN SHORT SUPPLY, A FENCE IS THE ANSWER.

Whether you are putting up a new fence where none exists, or replacing an existing fence because it is dilapidated, you need to do some homework before you start. There are three main areas you should think about.

Firstly, what sort of fence do you want? Looks are important, and you may need privacy or a barrier to keep children and pets in (or out); alternatively, you may want to hide garden eyesores like the compost heap, or provide an attractive backdrop for your display of plants.

Secondly, how much are you prepared to pay? Many people are surprised at how long their boundaries are (and hence at the likely cost, especially of the more expensive fencing types available).

Thirdly, are there any legal complications? Apart from the possibility of a dispute with your neighbours over ownership and boundary lines, there may be other legal restrictions on the way you fence in your property. See Legal considerations on page 10 for more details.

WHICH TYPE TO CHOOSE?

Most people think of timber when choosing a new fence, since there is a bigger choice in timber than in other materials. All timber fences are the same in principle. You put up a line of posts along the boundary line, and then fill the gaps in between with rails or panels.

The simplest type has one or more horizontal rails between the posts – known as **post-and-rail fencing**, or **ranch fencing** if the rails are flat boards. This type is fine as a boundary marker, but not much good at keeping pets or

children in (or out). You can make the fence a better barrier by adding vertical timbers to the horizontal rails; if you leave spaces between the verticals you get a **picket fence**, which is see-through but child and petproof, while overlapping them creates a **close-boarded** fence with complete privacy.

A variation on the ranch fencing idea has horizontal planks fixed to both sides of the posts so that the planks on one side coincide with the gaps on the other – this is known as **interference fencing**. There is a similar variation on picket fencing, with vertical timbers on both sides of the horizontal rails; this is generally called **interlap fencing**.

Panel fences differ from post-and-rail types in having made-up panels of various types fixed between the posts. These may be simple rustic affairs –

Right: Shaped pickets make a highly distinctive and decorative fence, while painted wood makes a contrasting formal planter.

agenda, whether it is to screen a patio or shelter tender plants. The same 'solid' fences that provide excellent privacy are one answer, but you must be sure that posts and panels are securely fixed to resist the buffeting the fence will receive from high winds. An alternative where total privacy is not so important is interference or interlap fencing, which allow air to pass between the opposed slats and so do not form such an impenetrable barrier to the wind as solid fences do.

Family security – keeping children and pets in or out – is another factor. The types already mentioned in this section will do a good job here, but if privacy is not important you could consider a high picket fence, chestnut palings or even open trelliswork. All will restrain small children and fat pets, but low types can be climbed fairly easily.

If you want to use your fence to **train climbing plants**, open trelliswork is the best, since eventually the plants will create a boundary with a completely natural look. Trellis also has the advantage of allowing light and water to reach the roots of the plants unhindered; solid fences sited to provide shelter may deprive plants on the leeward side of water and, depending on their orientation, sunlight too. If you use trellis, you must make sure that it is

---

Left: *The ultimate in simple garden woodwork – rustic poles for the fence and a reclaimed railway sleeper for a seat.*

Below: *Second-hand timber can also be put to use for more substantial structures.*

woven **willow hurdles**, for example, or stout wires carrying cleft **chestnut palings** or more elaborate (and more expensive) framed panels with **horizontal slats** (often waney-edged), **vertical boards** (similar in appearance to a traditional close-boarded fence, but minus the horizontal rails), **interwoven slats** of thin timber or even open **trelliswork**. These panels are generally made in a range of standard sizes; most are 1.8m (6ft) long, while heights range from a lowly 610mm (2ft) up to a more lofty 1.8m (6ft) tall.

POINTS TO PONDER

Apart from thinking purely about fence styles, there are other factors to consider when choosing your new fencing.

For most people, **privacy** is the most important. If you want to exclude prying eyes completely, you need a fence that is at least 1.8m (6ft) high, and your choice of types is restricted to vertical closeboarded types or solid panels.

Providing **shelter from prevailing winds** may also come high on the

FENCES

made from durable timber such as cedar, and that it is treated with preservative to keep rot at bay; future maintenance will be difficult once the plants have become established.

If all you want to do is mark a boundary, any type of fencing can be used. Probably the cheapest is a row of posts connected by either a single rail or lengths of ornamental chain.

Lastly, looks may matter, especially if you want your fencing to be unobtrusive. For example, high solid panel fences, unless softened by plants, can make a long, narrow garden look like a wood-panelled corridor, and white pickets and ranch-style fencing are very difficult to disguise – they are actually a strong garden feature in their own right.

Low fences tend to be less obtrusive, and the use of rustic poles and trellis helps to soften the effect still further. Remember, too, that leaving fences to weather to a natural grey colour can help them blend unobtrusively into the surroundings.

LEGAL CONSIDERATIONS

If you are replacing an existing fence, the first thing to do is to establish who owns it. The title deeds to your property may show this (on new developments, a T-mark on the site plans against a boundary lies on the property responsible for maintaining it). The old 'rule' that posts and rails are always on the owner's side is by no means infallible.

If you cannot establish ownership, try to come to a written and signed agreement with your neighbour, and keep it safe for future reference. If a dilapidated fence is his and he will not agree to repair or replace it, there is nothing to stop you from erecting a new fence on your side of the boundary line. Remember that you will need planning

permission in the UK to erect a fence over 2m (6ft 6in) high, except where the boundary faces a highway; then the height limit above which permission must be sought drops to 1m (3ft 3in). Hedges are not subject to planning permission. The Highways Acts may require you to lower a fence or hedge if it obstructs the view of motorists (usually only applicable on corner sites).

Lastly, your own deeds may contain restrictive covenants which curtail your right to erect certain types of fencing. For other countries, check your local regulations before proceeding.

BUYING FENCING

Fence prices vary widely from supplier to supplier, so the best advice is to shop around. The obvious places to buy fencing are from local fencing contractors, garden centres, builders' merchants or, for a restricted choice of the more popular types, do-it-yourself superstores. You will get the best choice from a fencing supplier. Remember that delivery may be extra, especially on

Above: Pickets cut to a profile that matches the elegant post tops and set on a gravel board cut a dashingly formal look.

Right: More pickets, this time marching smartly up hill and down dale to create an unusual formal boundary fence.

Top right: A simple post-and-rail fence makes an economical boundary marker where security is not an important factor.

Far right: Prefabricated panels provide the simplest and quickest way of putting up a fence.

10

small orders, and many 'trade' outlets quote prices without VAT. If you are in any doubt, ask.

When you are buying timber fences, check the wood quality carefully and try to avoid posts, rails and panels with splits or large numbers of knots. Make sure that all timber components have been preservative-treated either by pressure or vacuum impregnation, and that metal fittings have been galvanized or sherardised so they will not rust too quickly. Make sure that panel types have capping rails to shed rainwater, and buy caps for all the posts too.

PUTTING UP A TIMBER FENCE

The traditional way of putting up a fence is to set the posts in holes in the ground, and then to erect the rails, panels or whatever between them. The general rule of thumb is to bury one quarter of the post length in the ground, so for fencing 1.8m (6ft) high a post 2.4m (8ft) long is needed. You will find more detailed information about erecting posts on pages 88-89.

Above: *A horizontal closeboarded fence makes a sturdy peep-proof wind-break. The boards can have square or waney (untrimmed, often bark-covered) edges.*

LOOKING AFTER FENCES

The biggest enemy of timber fencing is neglect. Wind loosens posts and strains fixings; physical damage breaks rails and splits panels; rot attacks exposed endgrain and post bottoms. Regular treatment of all surfaces with wood preservative will help to keep rot at bay (see page 92), and regular inspection especially after periods of rough weather will help to pinpoint weakened fixings and loose posts before total collapse results.

Fix loose boards and panels by driving extra fixing nails into the rails or posts. Reinforce loose posts either by excavating round them and forming a concrete collar, or if rot has set in by fitting a concrete fence spur or a fence spike. See page 93 for more details.

CLOSE-BOARDED FENCES

The close-boarded fence is probably the finest fence you can build. It combines great strength with impressive good looks, and if carefully erected will give years of service. Its main drawback is that it uses a lot of solid wood, so tends to be more expensive than other types. However, one advantage that close-boarded fence has over other 'solid' fence types is that it can be built to follow a slope; you simply set out the

posts, add the rails parallel to the slope and nail the boards to them.

Its basic structure is quite simple: a line of posts connected by two or three arris rails depending on the fence height, with overlapping feather-edged boards nailed to the rails to complete the fence. In good quality work the arris rails are set in mortises cut in the posts, but nowadays galvanized metal brackets are more commonly used to secure the rails to the posts. The lower ends of the fence should rest on horizontal gravel boards which, as their name implies, prevent soil or gravel from being washed under the fence. They also stop rot from attacking the lower ends of the fence boards, which would otherwise be in contact with the ground. It is cheaper to replace a single rotten gravel board than a whole row of boards.

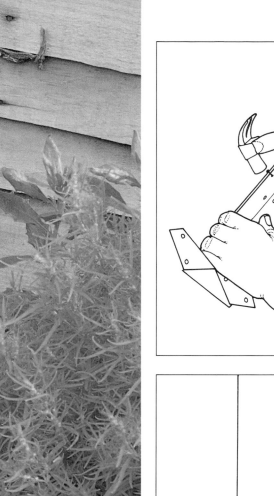

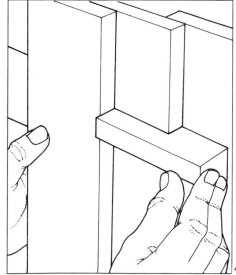

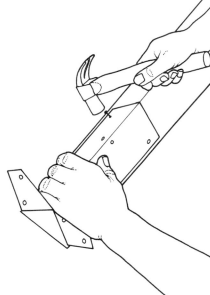

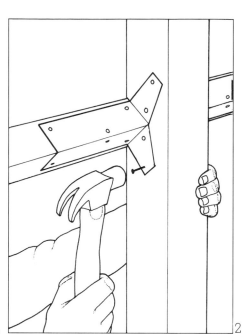

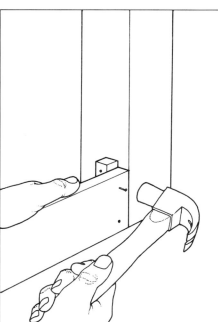

Erecting the fence

1 Once you have set out and erected the line of fence posts (see pages 88-89), measure the lengths of the arris rails needed to fit between each pair of posts and cut them to size. Nail an arris rail bracket to each end of the rails.

2 With a helper supporting the other end of the rail, drive nails through the angled flanges of the bracket to fix it to the fence. Fit all the rails, checking that they are parallel with the ground and, on three-rail fences, equally spaced.

3 Nail small cleats to the sides of each post to support the gravel rail with its face flush with the face of the post. Cut the gravel boards to length and then nail each one to its cleats. Set up a string line between the posts to help you get the tops of the boards level, about 75mm (3in) below the post tops. Cut the first board to length, set its lower end on the gravel board with its thicker edge against the post and check that its top is aligned with the string, then nail it to the upper rail by driving a nail through the board close to its thicker edge. Nail the board to the lower rail, and to the centre rail too if one is fitted. Nail on the second board so its thicker edge overlaps the thinner edge of the first board by about 12mm (1/2in). Drive the nails so they penetrate both boards.

4 Use a notched piece of scrap wood as a gauge to ensure a consistent overlap between adjacent boards.

5 Carry on nailing up boards, checking after every four or five boards that they are truly vertical using a spirit level. When you reach the next post, reverse the last board so its thicker edge is against the post and nail it in place. Complete the remaining bays of the fence in the same way, then add the post caps. Give the boards protection by fitting a bevelled capping strip.

FENCES

Right: Prefabricated panels can be made with overlapping waney-edged boards or thin interwoven strips.

PANEL FENCES

By comparison with the relative complexities of the close-boarded fence, a panel fence is simplicity itself. You simply nail prefabricated fence panels to the posts and finish off by adding the post caps. The result is not as sturdy as a boarded fence, since the panels are made from relatively thin wood with light-duty framing timbers. However, they are very quick to erect and are relatively inexpensive by comparison.

There are two points to remember when erecting panel fences. The first is that the post spacings must be very accurately matched to the panel width if gaps or buckled panels are to be avoided. The second is that they obviously cannot be used on sloping ground unless they top a wall that can follow the ground slope in a series of steps.

1 Since fence panels are a standard width, it is vital that the posts are accurately spaced to match the panel size. Use a batten cut to match the panel width as an aid to positioning the posts to precisely the right separation.
2 With the posts set in place, position the first panel between its posts, resting on bricks or timber offcuts to lift the panel just clear of the ground. Drive fixing nails at 300mm (12in) intervals.
3 Alternatively, use galvanized panel brackets – two per side on low fences, three on high ones.
4 Slot the panel into place and drive nails in through the bracket holes.
5 If you need a narrow panel to fill in the last section of the fence run, prise off the outer frame battens and reposition them to form a panel of the required width. Drive fixing nails through the upper batten so they pass through the lower one and hammer their points flat. Cut down the panel alongside the repositioned battens, then test its fit and nail it into place between its posts.

PICKET FENCING

The picket fence, with its closely-spaced row of vertical timbers, is perfectly redolent of the thatched country cottage with roses round the door. It is a style traditionally used for low fences, often with a hedge planted immediately inside it, and looks especially effective against dark foliage if painted white. The tops of the individual pickets are usually rounded or arrowheaded, but there is nothing to stop you from being more artistically creative and cutting spade or club shapes, forming pierced cutouts and so on, if you have the time. Pigmented wood stains are a better finish than paint if you want to avoid regular tedious redecorating.

Once you have decided on the post spacing and set up the posts, cut the rails to length so you can work out how many pickets you will need for each bay. Cut all the pickets to length and shape.

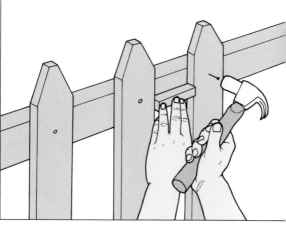

1 Nail the pickets to the rails using an offcut of wood as a spacer to ensure that the gaps are uniform

4 | 5

2 Use wooden cleats to secure the rails to the posts. Screw them to the post sides first, then screw through the rails into the cleats.

FENCES

POST-AND-RAIL FENCES

Post-and-rail fences, as their name implies, consist of a row of posts linked by horizontal rails with gaps between them. They can be made from sawn or planed timber, which gives them a sleek appearance suitable for a modern house with a neatly regimented garden, or from rustic poles which look more natural and suit the rambling style of a more well-established garden. However, unless the rails are closely spaced the fence is not particularly secure, and all types can be easily climbed so they are perhaps best avoided when you want to keep inquisitive children in. With rustic poles, you can embellish the fence and improve security a little by using shorter pieces to create infill panels between the posts.

If economy and boundary marking are all you require of a fence, chestnut palings could be the best choice. These are slim split poles linked together by strands of galvanized wire to form a 'fence on a roll'. All you have to do is to unroll it, cut it to length and secure the wires to your fence posts with stout staples or bent-over nails.

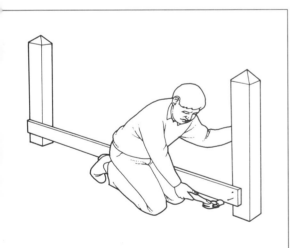

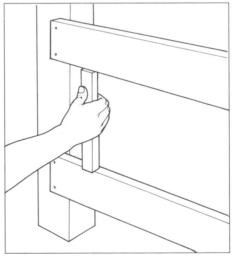

Above: Closely spaced rustic poles form a natural looking, yet very secure fence.

1 With your posts in position, start by nailing the lowest rail to the posts.
2 Use offcuts as spacers when nailing on the second and subsequent rails to ensure uniform gaps between them.
3 On level ground, use a spirit level to check that the rails are truly horizontal and parallel with each other. To create interference fencing, nail more rails to the other side of the posts in line with the gaps on this side.

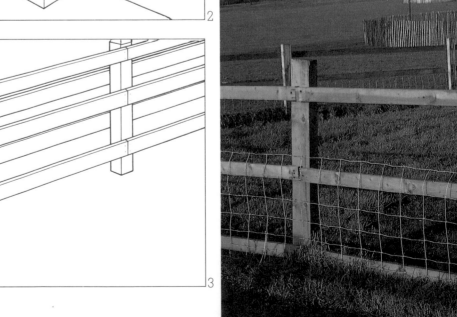

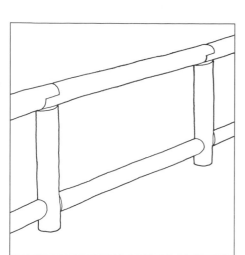

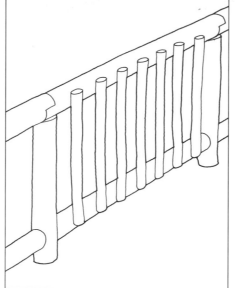

1 Start by nailing stout poles to the tops and sides of the posts to form the main horizontal rails of the fence. Drive the nails in at opposing angles.

2 If you want a relatively solid fence, nail closely-spaced slimmer poles to the rails. Support these from behind as you drive the fixing nails.

3 To create a decorative effect, use short lengths of slim pole cut with angled ends to form geometrical designs between the posts and the main rails.

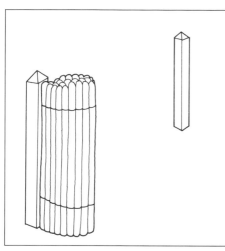

1 Set out the fence posts at the required spacing, then unroll the paling bundle along the fence run. Check that all the poles are securely held by the wires.

2 Stand the fencing up against the posts and secure one end of the length to the first post using stout galvanised wire staples hammered well into the post.

3 Go to the next post and pull the length taut, then secure it to the post. Continue along the run, removing any unwanted section with wire cutters.

Left: Horizontal rails nailed to posts look smart, but can be climbed very easily. Add wire mesh for extra security.

Above: Chestnut paling makes an excellent temporary boundary and is easy to put up and take down.

GATES

GATES CAN MARK THE ENTRANCE TO YOUR PROPERTY, DETER PROWLERS FROM ENTERING YOUR BACK GARDEN OR KEEP CHILDREN IN AND STRAY ANIMALS OUT. THEY COME IN A WIDE RANGE OF STYLES, MATERIALS AND SIZES, RANGING FROM A LOW BARRIER SET IN A FRONT FENCE TO IMPOSING ENTRANCE GATES, OFTEN HUNG IN PAIRS, FOR VEHICLES. THE MOST POPULAR MATERIAL IS WITHOUT DOUBT TIMBER, AND THE GATE IS OFTEN MADE TO MATCH THE STYLE OF ANY ADJACENT FENCING.

The most important part of any gate is the gate posts, which must be strong enough to carry the gate's weight without allowing it to sag. You can hang your gate from timber posts, often available from the gate supplier, or you can build more permanent brick piers at each side of the opening.

You are likely to choose a gate for one of three positions: as a pedestrian entrance gate at the front of your property, as a side gate to bar access round the house to the back garden, or as a vehicle entrance to a driveway. Front gates – whether for pedestrians or cars – are generally around 1m (3ft 3in) high (you may need planning permission for a higher gate and fence on a boundary fronting a road). Widths range from about 1m for single front gates up to about 4m (13ft) for single barred field gates. Double gates can span drives as narrow as 2m (6ft 6in) and openings as wide as 6m (20ft). Side gates are usually 2m (6ft 6in) high and 1m wide.

CHOOSING MATERIALS

Most wooden gates are made of softwood – usually larch – which has been pretreated with preservative to keep rot at bay. More expensive gates in woods like oak and cedar have better resistance to rot and insect attack, but are more expensive.

Timber gate posts are also either preservative-treated softwood or oak (the latter are preferable, though they

Above: *A gate can be as individual as its owner, and will certainly help callers to recognise where you live!*

Below: *Nothing looks smarter than crisp white paint on a front gate, especially when it matches the house paintwork.*

cost more). Choose 100mm (4in) posts for low single gates, and 125 or 150mm (5 or 6in) posts for high side gates and wide drive gates. As far as post length is concerned, you need to bury about 450mm (18in) of post in the ground for a single gate 1m high, and 600mm (2ft) for a gate 2m high. For double gates, increase the buried depth to a minimum depth of 750mm (2ft 6in).

Many gates are hung between brick piers, either standing alone or as part of a boundary wall. They should be at least one brick (215mm) square for 1m-high gates, and 1½ bricks (330mm) square for higher or wider gates, and must be built on firm foundations. If you are building the piers up before hanging the gate, you can build in the hinge supports as the pier rises; alternatively, you can attach face-fixing plates direct to the brickwork, or even fit timber battens to the piers to carry the fixings. This last method is a useful way of making a standard width gate fit an opening that is a little too wide for it.

FOUNDATIONS

Good foundations are essential to keep gate posts upright and secure, or to support brick piers. It is best to set posts for side and narrow entrance gates in a continuous foundation, with the concrete securing the two posts linked by a strip of concrete about 200mm (8in) thick across the opening. This prevents the hinge post from being pulled inward by the gate's movement. Each post should be set in a concrete collar about 150mm (6in) deep, in a hole around 300mm (12in) across and deep enough to accept the necessary buried length of the gate post.

Brick piers should be built on a concrete pad twice the size of the pier for low gates, three times the size for high ones. It should be at least 150mm (6in) thick. Use a 1:2:3 sand:cement:aggregate mix for the footings, and leave to set for at least seven days before building the piers.

Above: *You can echo your house's colour scheme on your front fence and entrance gate too.*

HANGING A GATE

The most important stage is working out how far apart the posts should be, and to do this you should lay the gate and the posts flat on the ground (with the gate supported on battens to raise it level with the rear face of the post to which the hinges will be attached). Then lay the hinges and catch in position, and adjust the gap between gate and posts to give adequate clearance. Mark a depth line across each post about 75mm (3in) below the bottom of the gate to act as a guide when setting them in the ground.

Check with a tape measure to ensure that the posts are parallel, and then pin three battens (two at right angles, one diagonal) to the posts to hold them the right distance apart.

GATES

Next, mark the gate post positions on the ground, and dig out a hole for each post to about 50mm (2in) more than the required depth. Link the two holes with a trench about 200mm (8in) deep if the posts are 1m or less apart. Lay some gravel or well-broken hardcore in the base of each hole, and set the linked posts in place. Tap them down until the depth marks coincide with ground level; then pin angled struts to each post to hold it precisely vertical, by checking with your spirit level.

You can now pack in more hardcore to within about 150mm (6in) of the surface, and pour in the concrete (a fairly dry mix of 1 part cement to 5 parts combined aggregate). Tamp this down well to form a collar round the posts,

Right: *Even the simplest gate can be the focal point of the façade, if treated to a splash of colour.*

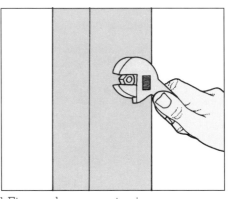

1 Fix wooden spacer to pier.

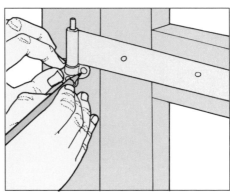

4 Fit upper hinge and hinge cup.

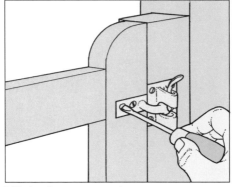

5 Fit latch to gate and post.

2 Offer up hinge and mark holes.

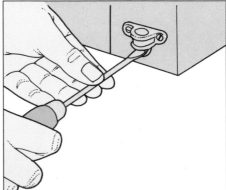

3 Fit lower hinge cups.

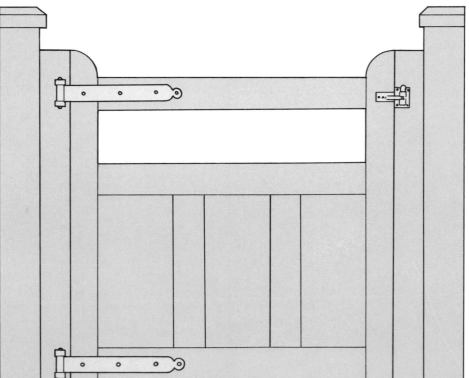

taking care not to knock them off line, and slope the surface away from the post faces to aid drainage. Then lay more concrete in the trench between the post holes to consolidate the whole setting. Leave the concrete to harden round the posts for 48 hours before removing the struts and braces.

Prop the gate between the posts on bricks or timber offcuts, and use timber wedges to centre it between them. For flush hinges, set the gate's inner face flush with the rear of the posts; for pintype fittings, centre the gate between the front and rear faces of the posts.

Now hold each fitting in place against the gate and mark the positions of the fixing screws. Most gates are hung with tee or reversible hinges; make sure that the strap of the hinge is centred on the gate's horizontal rails, and if the gate has a diagonal brace make sure that it runs up from the hinged edge, not down towards it. Drill

pilot holes and attach the fittings – initially with just a couple of screws, so you can test the gate's operation before driving in the rest. Make sure that catches and automatic latches work easily, and reposition them slightly if they do not.

Heavy, wide timber gates are usually hung on strap hinges and suspended from pins that are bolted through the post for extra strength. Fit the pins to the posts first, then prop up the gate so you can mark the strap positions.

You can add a range of 'optional extras' to your gate to make it more convenient to use. These include self-closing springs and automatic latches, hold-backs (to hold the gate in the open position) and bolts for additional security. These can engage in keepers mounted on the gate posts or, for double gates across a driveway, in a stop block set in the ground. You can add padlocks or locking chains for extra security.

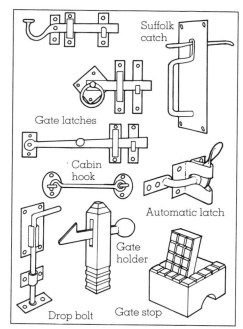

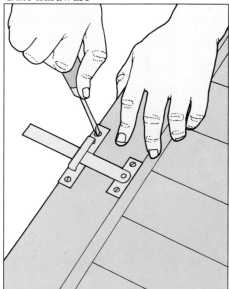

Gate hardware

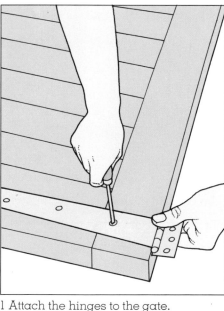

1 Attach the hinges to the gate.

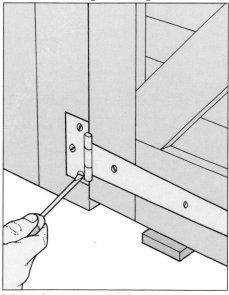

2 Prop the gate and attach the hinges.

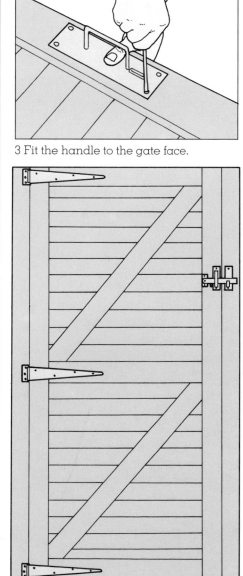

3 Fit the handle to the gate face.

4 Attach the latch to the gate.

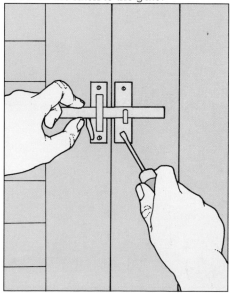

5 Fit the keeper to the post.

Pergolas and Walkways

Free-standing arches form an attractive feature of any garden, especially where there are distinct zones – lawn and vegetable garden for example – and can be built easily in a variety of materials to provide a sturdy framework for plants such as climbing roses. Pergolas are just a series of linked arches built to create a pleasant walkway – down the side of the garden, for example, or across it to shade a patio or sitting-out area – which offer more scope for displaying climbing and trailing plants to good effect.

The most popular material used for garden arches and pergolas is the rustic pole – the trimmed stem of a slender sapling (usually larch) up to about 75mm (3in) in diameter, with or without its bark – but you can build these structures equally well using sawn or planed timber, perhaps in conjunction with brick piers, or by using metal hoops (home-made or prefabricated). Individual plant supports can be provided by incorporating guide wires or by adding sections of trelliswork to the structure.

Arches and pergolas are available in kit form – the perfect answer for the gardener in a hurry – but the big advantage of building your own is the control you have over size, shape and style. The job is pleasingly simple, especially if you go for an all-timber construction, and the end result will be an attractive addition to your garden. Either way, you have the pleasure of designing the support and choosing and training the plants that will make it your own.

Left: *Planed and stained timber makes the perfect pergola for this walled patio.*

Choosing the Size

Overall size matters relatively little where arches and pergolas are concerned, although you obviously want to keep some sense of scale. A huge pergola could spoil the proportions of a small garden, while a puny little arch in the middle of an acre of lawn would appear quite ridiculous. It is a good idea to have a close look at what friends and neighbours have achieved in their gardens before finalizing your own plans.

There are some practical minimum dimensions to bear in mind as far as width and height are concerned, however. You need enough clearance between the uprights of arches and pergolas not only to allow you to walk easily, but also to allow you to push a wheelbarrow through without the foliage snagging clothes or skin. For an

arch, around 1.2m (4ft) between the uprights is usually adequate, while a pergola can be much wider if you wish. As far as height is concerned, 2.1m (7ft) is a sensible minimum for both arches and pergolas, and you should increase this to 2.4m (8ft) if you plan to grow trailing plants over them.

DESIGN FEATURES

The actual design of your arch or pergola is entirely up to you. Rustic poles are generally formed into simple rectangular frames with diagonal cross-braces, while sawn or planed timber looks best with the roof members projecting over the 'walls', since this allows trailing plants to hang freely without obstructing the walkway. For a pergola, aim to have an upright post every 1m (3ft 3in) or thereabouts.

PREPARING THE SITE

Wherever you plan to site your arch or pergola, the first step is to ensure that there are no overhead obstructions –

tree branches are the most obvious candidate for trimming. Next, clear away unwanted vegetation from each side of the opening if you are building an arch, and around each post position for a pergola.

If the site is covered with loose-laid paving slabs or bricks, lift units to allow you to position your uprights; they can be cut to size and replaced later. With concrete and mortared-in paving (crazy paving, for example), either chip holes in the surface so you can sink your posts or use surface-mounted sockets to support them.

CHOOSING MATERIALS

If you are planning an all-timber construction, your choice lies between rustic poles and sawn or planed timber.

Rustic poles look best in an informal cottage-style garden. Choose poles with a base diameter of around 75mm (3in) for posts, plus some slimmer poles for cross-braces and infill members. Most are sold with the bark on, but you can easily strip this off if you prefer a 'bare'

look (the weather will remove the dead bark anyway in time). Garden centres are the best source of supply, although in rural areas local farmers and even the Forestry Commission may be worth contacting too.

Sawn and planed timber creates a more formal effect, although you can still make your constructions blend in unobtrusively if you can find some well-weathered wood to use. For arches, posts should be of 75mm (3in) square timber, while pergola uprights should be 100mm (4in) square for extra strength, and main side bearers should be 100 x 50mm (4 x 2in). Other arch rails and braces can be of 50mm (2in) square wood, while pergola 'joists' can be 75 x 50mm (3 x 2in) or even 75 x 38mm (3 x 1½in), set on edge. All wood should be pre-treated with preservative, unless you are using a naturally rot-resistant wood such as cedar, so fencing suppliers or specialist timber merchants are probably the best source of materials.

Apart from the wood, you will also need some concrete (or metal fence spikes for square posts) to set the uprights in place, plus 100mm (4in) long galvanized nails to secure the joints and some extra preservative to treat cut ends. For pergolas with brick piers, add some galvanized angle brackets plus fixing screws and wallplugs for securing the main bearers to the masonry.

If you are planning to set your pergola on masonry piers rather than on timber posts, you can choose brick,

Pergolas and Walkways

reconstituted stone walling blocks or even the pilaster blocks sold with pierced screen block walling (which could itself be laid between the piers). Brick is the cheapest material to use, especially if you can get hold of some well-weathered second-hand ones, but you need a reasonable level of brick-laying skill to get good results.

Right: *This simply constructed walkway has become a feature of the garden thanks to a clever planting scheme.*

Below right: *Rustic poles are used to good effect to create this simple archway between two garden zones.*

Below: *This elegant pergola has been designed to span the whole of the garden, with planting beds between the formally laid paths.*

Reconstituted stone walling blocks are easier to handle for ham-fisted bricklay-ers, since even jointing is not so critical, but they are more expensive than bricks. Screen wall pilaster blocks with hollow centres are the easiest of all to build up, but the pier must be built around a steel reinforcing rod set in the pier foundation and the centre of the column must be filled with concrete. Whichever material you choose, builders' merchants are likely to be the best (and cheapest) source of supply.

Brick-and-wood Pergolas

If you plan to have masonry piers to support your pergola, you must first of all lay concrete foundation pads at each pier position. These should be about 450mm (18in) square and at least 100mm (4in) thick, laid over 75mm (3in) of well-rammed hardcore. If the piers will rise off an existing concrete or rigidly-paved surface, no further foun-

Above: A pergola that is well-clad with foliage can also create the ideal shaded sitting-out area for hot sunny days.

---

dation will be needed, but slabs and pavers laid on sand are not a strong enough base and must be lifted so a foundation pad can be laid. Where pilaster blocks are being used, set an L-shaped starter bar of 16mm (5/8in) diameter deformed steel (available from builders' merchants) in the foundation and then tie more steel bar or 50mm (2in) angle iron to it with a 500mm (20in) overlap using galvanized wire.

Build up brick and block piers 1½ units square; with bricks this gives a pier 330mm (13in) square, while the size of a block pier will depend on the basic block size.

When the piers reach the desired height, set the main 100 x 50mm (4 x 2in) wall plates in place on top and secure them with galvanized angle brackets screwed to drilled and plugged holes in the pier tops. Then measure the span across the pergola and notch the cross rails so they fit over the main wall plates at each end, and secure them in place

with nails driven in at an angle. Finish off by treating all the woodwork with a coat of non-toxic preservative.

PLANED TIMBER PERGOLAS

Whatever design you choose for a timber pergola of this sort, you should start by setting the uprights in position. Post spacing isn't critical – a 1m (3ft 3in) gap is about right, but you could increase this to 1.2m (4ft) if you prefer.

On open ground, you can either set the posts in concrete or use metal fence spikes (quicker to use, but less sturdy with tall posts). If you are using concrete, you need to set at least 450mm (18in) of post in the ground, so make sure you can get posts long enough.

If you are using fence spikes, you simply drive them into the ground with an offcut of post timber placed in the socket to protect it; then discard the offcut, set the post in the socket and secure it with nails or screws. Although these spikes offer a quick fixing, it can be difficult to get the spikes truly vertical, especially in stony soil.

On existing concrete and rigid paved surfaces, it is probably easier to secure

the posts with special post shoes which are fixed in place with masonry bolts.

Once the posts are in place, let the concrete set. Then either notch the tops of the posts to accept the main bearer rails at each side of the pergola, or simply nail them to the faces of the posts. Finally, add the cross rails as described earlier for a brick-and-timber pergola. See pages 29-31 for more details on pergola construction.

RUSTIC PERGOLAS

It is much easier to build arches and pergolas using rustic poles than it is using masonry and sawn or planed timber, because you do not have to take so much care over the assembly; many of the joints are simply overlapped and nailed together, and any genuine joints are only half-laps.

You can build a rustic arch in two ways – either by setting the posts in place first and then adding the cross-rails, braces and arch head as shown on pages 26-27, or by making up the side and top panels first and then setting each side panel in place as one unit before adding the top panel.

Pergolas and Walkways

If you plan some pre-assembly, select your uprights and lay them flat on the ground. Then position the main cross-rails and braces across the posts, marking the joint positions with tape when you are happy with them. To form the joints, either saw down the sides of each cut-out and chisel out the waste to form halving joints, or else make a rounded cut-out in one member to accept the rounded surface of the other. Apply a liberal dose of preservative to all cut surfaces before final assembly. Then secure the joints with galvanized nails driven in at opposing angles for extra strength.

You can now position each side frame, setting the two posts in concrete and bracing each side panel upright while the concrete sets. When it has, nail or screw the arch head sections into place to complete the construction.

1 Start by marking the positions of the pergola uprights on the ground – a handful of sand makes an ideal marker – and check that you are starting out with everything square by measuring the diagonals between the corner posts. They will be equal if the base layout is square or rectangular.

Then dig out the holes to a depth of about 450mm (18in). You can check on progress by standing the post in the hole, laying a cane across it at ground level and marking this level on the post. Dig down a further 75mm (3in) or so and set a brick in the base of the hole on which to stand the pole when you come to set it in place.

You can secure the posts either by surrounding them with a collar of concrete, as though you were putting up fence posts, or by sinking short sections of clay drain pipe in the ground to act as post sockets (the posts are later wedged firmly into the sockets by trickling sand

into the pipes round the posts), The advantage of the latter method over direct concreting is that you can more easily replace a rotten post if necessary in the future.

If you go for direct concreting, stand the post upright on its brick and brace it in position with two lengths of scrap wood nailed to the post at about 45° to the ground and set at right angles to each other. Their other ends simply rest on the ground or can be weighted with bricks on paved surfaces.

Next, mix up the concrete to a dryish consistency, shovel it in round the base of the post and tamp it down with a post offcut. Finish the concrete about 75mm (3in) below the surrounding ground level. This allows soil or turf to be replaced round the post when the construction is completed.

If you prefer the socket method, use the same technique as for concreting posts to set the socket in place in the ground. Here the top of the socket should be at ground level, with the concrete stopping about 75mm below it.

With sockets, put a post in and check with a spirit level that it is standing truly vertical before you finish concreting in the socket. Use pressure on the post to change the position of the socket slightly if necessary.

Complete the groundwork by placing and concreting all the other sockets or posts, and leave them overnight for the concrete to harden. Do not remove the braces until it has done so.

2 Next, mark the height you want the pergola to be on the uprights, and saw them to length. It is better to fit slightly over-long posts to begin with and cut

them to size than to try to install cut-to-length posts precisely the same depth in the ground. One will always finish up a little shorter than its neighbours.

Before proceeding with the rest of the pergola structure, treat the cut ends of the posts with preservative to provide some additional protection against rot. Also treat all cuts and joints you make in the other components of the pergola with preservative as you cut them.

Use a bowsaw and chisel to shape simple joints in the cross-rails. You can either use the saw on its own to make roughly semi-circular cut-outs which will accept the rounded surface of the adjacent frame member, or else use a broad chisel as well to cut square

4

6

5

right angles to the first, again shaping simple joints first and then nailing down through the joint into the rail below. Make sure that the second lot of nails miss those securing the lower rail to the post top.

At this stage you can also add intermediate cross rails to give the structure a 'roof' if you want plants to climb across the pergola as well as up it.

Next, offer up shorter poles for use as struts so you can mark the post and rail angles on them. They look best set at 45° angles to the posts, but you can fit them at other angles if you prefer.

Saw or chisel the ends of the struts to the required angles. If you make the cut concave across the width of the pole, it will fit more positively against the posts and rails and the joint will look more natural than it will if the cuts are made squarely.

6 Check each strut for fit, and trim the length or alter the angle if necessary to get a good fit against the adjacent posts and rails.

Drive the fixing nails partway through each end of the strut, then hold it up and use an offcut of pole to knock it into place before hammering the nails fully home. Do not place the nails too close to the angled ends of the struts or they may split as you fix them in place.

You can also add horizontal braces between the top rails at the corners of the pergola to increase its rigidity and to provide additional support for climbing plants.

halving joints in each component so that they interlock. The latter makes for a stronger structure, but takes a little longer.

3 Fix the the first set of rails to the posts by nailing down through the joint. Here a semi-circular cut-out in the top of each post creates a positive location for the rail. Use galvanized nails for all the fixings so they will not rust away. If any nails points completely penetrate the rails, hammer them over so they cannot

injure anyone (this is called clench nailing, and actually strengthens the structure because the hooked nail cannot be pulled out by high winds).

4 If the rails are not long enough to span the whole structure from side to side, cut them long enough to reach about 50mm (2in) past the next post. Then use your bowsaw again to make simple spliced joints above the post and nail down through the joint into the post top.

5 Add the second set of cross-rails at

Above: *Rustic poles make a natural support framework for climbing roses along a walkway leading to the rose garden itself.*

With the structure of the pergola complete, go round and check that all the joints are securely nailed, that no nail points are protruding anywhere and that all joints and cut ends have been treated with at least two coats of wood preservative.

Next, backfill round concreted posts and clay pipe sockets with soil, and trickle sand into the sockets to lock the posts securely into position inside them.

Finally, staple lengths of galvanized training wires across the structure to provide additional support for climbing plants. Alternatively, you can fix up pieces of trellis – ideal if you want one side of the pergola to be relatively peep proof once it is clothed in vegetation. Make sure that the panels are securely fixed to support the weight of the foliage.

PREFABRICATED KITS

If all this do-it-yourself activity is too much for you, you may prefer to opt for a pergola or arch in kit form. Some are of timber, closely resembling the types discussed here, but most kits have metal frame members which are simply set in place – either by driving the uprights into the ground directly, or by setting them in concrete as for DIY types. Assembly is quite straightforward.

Left: *A pergola in its infancy, waiting for nature to catch up. Now is the time for thorough preservative treatment.*

BUILDING A PLANED TIMBER PERGOLA

The step-by-step construction shown here covers all the basic steps involved in building a pergola using standard off-the-peg sawn timber. Follow them carefully whether you wish to copy this particular design or decide to experiment with one of your own. The resulting structure will be sturdy enough to support even the most luxuriant plant cover, yet is relatively unobtrusive as a garden feature.

If you do want to build a variation on this theme, it is a simple matter to alter the proportions of the pergola shown to make it longer – to serve as a walkway along a path, for example – or wider. In the former case, increase the depth of the cross rails by 25 or 50mm (1 or 2in) to prevent them from sagging over a wider span; in the latter, simply add on extra bays – additional pairs of posts, extended side rails and a further set of cross rails – to the length you want.

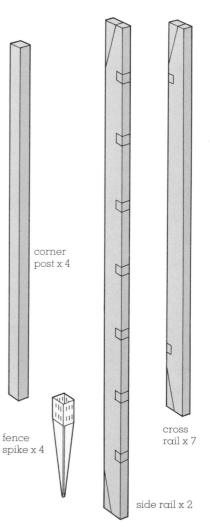

corner
post x 4

fence
spike x 4

cross
rail x 7

side rail x 2

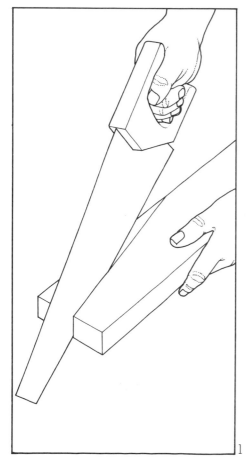

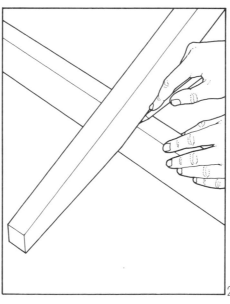

1 Cut the side and cross rails to length, then use a panel or rip saw to make the sloping cuts at each end of the rails.
2 Lay the side rails and two cross rails on the ground with a 300mm (12in) overhang at each corner. Measure the diagonals to ensure that the frame is square. Mark the positions of the cross rails on the top edges of the side rails at each corner, ready for the halving joints to be cut in each component.

Pergolas and Walkways

Use 75mm (3in) square planed or sawn timber for the four corner posts and 100 x 50mm (4 x 2in) wood for the two side rails and seven cross rails. Set the posts in 75mm fence spikes, or bed them in concrete (see pages 88-89 for more details of the technique).

The rails are assembled using simple halving joints cut in each component, and each side and end cross rail is secured to the posts with 6mm ($\frac{1}{4}$in) coach screws. The intermediate cross rails are secured to the side rails with coach screws driven in through their top edges.

Buy only preservative-treated timber, and give the whole structure – especially cut ends and joints – extra protection with a further coat of preservative.

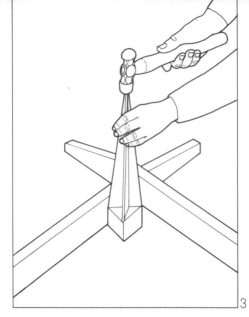

corner posts

fence spike

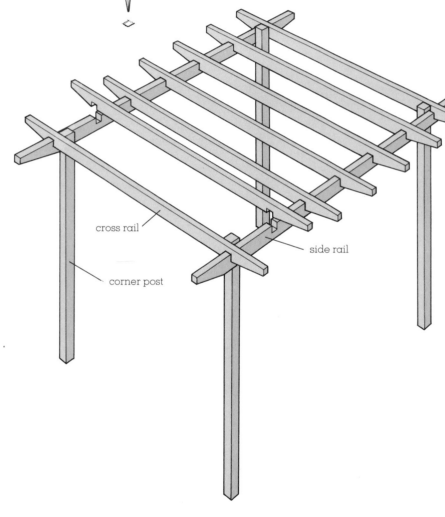

cross rail

side rail

corner post

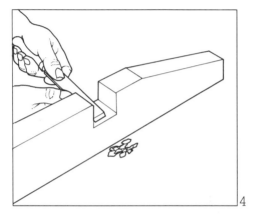

3

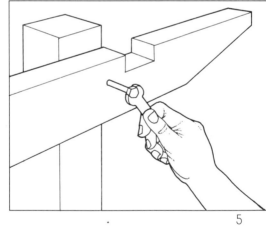

4

5

6

3 Hold a post offcut or an inverted fence spike in each corner of the frame and strike it with a hammer to mark the post positions on the ground. If you are using fence spikes, drive them in at the marked positions using a mallet, with an offcut of post timber in the socket to protect it. If you are using concrete, excavate each hole and put some hardcore in the bottom. Brace the posts upright, check their positions and tamp in the concrete.
4 Mark out the halving joints on the rails

by squaring lines down their sides to their midpoints and adding a depth line. Cut the sides of each joint with a tenon saw down to the depth line, then chisel out the waste to leave a slot.
5 Drill 6mm ($\frac{1}{4}$in) pilot holes through each rail 38mm from the halving joints. Use 6mm coach screws to secure the side and end cross rails to the posts.
6 Drill holes through each cross rail, and screw them to the posts. Check that everything is square and tighten up the screws with a spanner.

Right: A simple patio pergola can be made to seem like an extension to the building if decorated to match the house colour scheme.

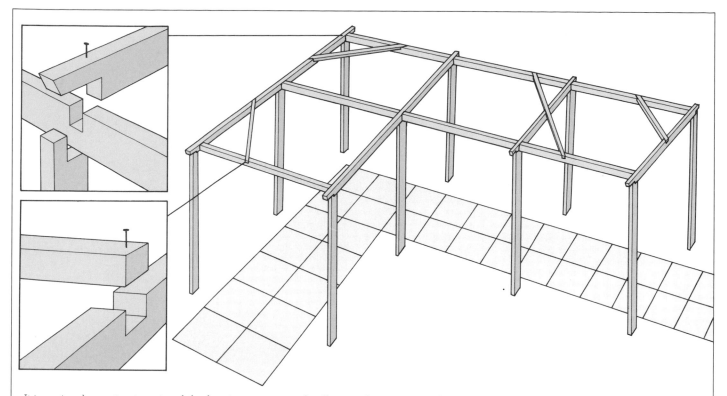

It is a simple matter to extend the basic pergola structure shown on page 30 to create a walkway that can run along a path and even turn corners. The diagonal roof braces are an alternative means of stiffening the structure if trellis or training wires are to be used to support the plants instead of roof slats. The details show how the tops of the posts are cut away to provide a positive location for the side rails, which are in turn notched to accept the transverse rails. Simple nailed joints like these also help give the structure additional rigidity.

Roofing a pergola

The natural cladding for a pergola is of course climbing plants, and if you add cross rails, training wires or trellis panels to the structure you will soon encourage them to form a natural roof. However, if you want quicker results or you need a structure that provides a greater degree of shade and shelter, there are a couple of other 'roofing' options you could consider.

The first is to provide a roof that keeps off the rain but lets in the light, and for this rigid plastic sheet is the best answer

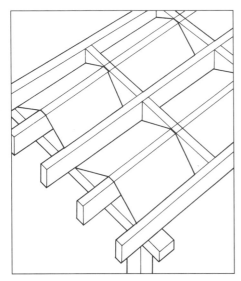

Above: *You can add temporary shading to a pergola simply by draping opaque fabric over and under the joists and tacking or stapling it into place.*

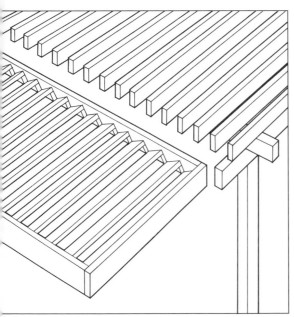

Above: *Closely-spaced slats provide some shade when the sun is not directly overhead. You can create more shade by angling the slats like louvres.*

- not the flimsy and ugly corrugated type, but so-called twin-wall polycarbonate sheeting which is widely used nowadays as a low-cost alternative to safety glass for conservatory roofs. Obviously you cannot use this successfully with a rustic pergola because of the uneven nature of the individual poles, but it is ideal for pergolas constructed with sawn or planed timber.

To support the individual panes, nail 25mm (1in) square battens to the inner sides of the roof beams so they slope slightly downwards. Then cut the panes to size with a fine-toothed saw and lay them in place on the battens. If you want the roof to be waterproof, pipe a bead of non-setting mastic along the top edge of all the battens first and press the sheet down into it to seal the edges. Then nail on more square battens to the roof beams above the panes to sandwich them securely in place. Repeat the process for the other bays of the roof.

The second option provides temporary shade from the sun, but not a waterproof shelter. It involves using roller blinds in an unconventional way, running them horizontally between the beams that make up the roof of the pergola rather than in their more usual vertical mode of operation. Remember that it is essential to use waterproofed awning material for this, not interior blind fabric which will soon become waterlogged and will then rot.

The blind is made up to suit the width of each bay of the roof, and is fixed in position by screwing the standard roller support brackets to the inner face of one of the side beams. To support it when it is extended lengths of plant-training

Below: *This ingenious arrangement of horizontal roller blinds provides shade for the patio when it is needed and can be rolled back when it is not.*

wire are fixed between the transverse beams, just below the blind roller position. To extend the blind, a cord is fitted to the draw bar and runs across the bay to the opposite side, where it is taken over a pulley and drops to a cleat on one of the pergola posts. The cord is freed from its cleat and pulled down to extend the blind, which runs out across its supporting wire as far as is needed to shade the area below; the cord is then tied off to the cleat. When you want to retract the blind again, you simply release the cord from the cleat and allow the roller spring to pull the blind back onto its roller again.

Right: *Here a basic pergola structure has been fitted with a glazed roof to provide a covered but well-lit walkway.*

Below: *Roofing your pergola with trellis-work creates attractive shadows.*

TRELLIS

TRELLISWORK, USUALLY IN THE FORM OF AN OPEN LATTICE MADE FROM SLIM TIMBER LATHS, IS ONE OF THE MOST VERSATILE AND INEXPENSIVE OF GARDEN FEATURES. IT IS MOST COMMONLY USED AS A SUPPORT FOR CLIMBING PLANTS, BUT CAN BE A SIMPLE VISUAL SCREEN IN ITS OWN RIGHT, ESPECIALLY IN ITS MORE ORNATE DECORATIVE FORMS. IT CAN BE FIXED TO WALLS AS A WAY OF SCREENING UGLY FEATURES OF A BUILDING, OR SUPPORTED ON POSTS TO FORM A TRELLIS FENCE. IT CAN EVEN BE USED TO FORM THE WALLS AND ROOFS OF GARDEN BUILDINGS, WHERE ITS OPEN STRUCTURE ALLOWS SUNLIGHT TO FORM INTERESTING PATTERNS OF LIGHT AND SHADE ON THE FLOOR SURFACE INSIDE.

Trelliswork offers almost endless variety to the creative gardener. In its most basic form it consists of a square or diamond-shaped grid of slim wooden laths nailed or stapled together and sometimes fitted with a perimeter frame to hold the lattice in its formation and to make it easier to handle and mount.

The grid size can vary too; most ready-made trellis panels have a 100mm (4in) grid repeat, but if you are making up your own trellis it can be smaller or larger than this. Remember that the smaller the grid size, the more rigid the trellis will be. A small grid will also appear more 'solid' and visually intrusive than will a larger size....but this may well be the effect you want to achieve anyway.

The basic trellis format is of course open to all sorts of design adaptations. The simplest is to use single pins to secure the overlapping laths, allowing the square grid to be deformed into a diamond shape. This is essential if you want to use trellis on a sloping site – atop a boarded fence, for example, or to screen a flight of steps. As you make up the grid, you can mix large and small squares, set some as lozenge shapes

enough when you first put it up, but once plants have grown up the trellis it may have to support a considerable weight of foliage and must be fixed securely enough to withstand high winds without collapsing. Since the fixings between individual laths are not particularly strong, the combination of framing and good support is essential.

There are two other factors to bear in mind when making and fitting trellis. The first is that once it is in position and plants have started to grow up it you will have great difficulty in maintaining or decorating it. To get round this potential problem, either use wood such as cedar which is naturally resistant to decay or buy preservative-treated wood and treat it liberally with more preservative after making the trellis panels up; pay special attention to the cut ends, leaving them standing in preservative overnight after cutting but before final assembly so the liquid can penetrate deep into the end grain. If you want your trellis coloured rather than *au naturel*, use pigmented wood stains or microporous paint rather than conventional outdoor paints, which will soon begin to crack, peel and look generally unsightly behind the foliage.

The second problem concerns not the trellis, but any wall against which you decide to fix it. As with the point made earlier about maintenance, a fully clothed trellis will effectively prevent you from reaching the masonry behind. Brickwork should not need any remedial work anyway so long as its pointing is in good condition, but if the wall

Above: *Trellis makes a stunning fencing material in its own right.*

Left: *Trellis lines the walls of this court-yard, and has also been used to surround the flower beds.*

Right: *Another example of trellis used as a design feature, here to form a frame behind a statue.*

within outer squares, and add diagonals and other details as you wish. There is no reason why you should not use laths of different thicknesses for different areas of the design. You can even create curves if the laths you use are thin enough to be bent without splitting (soak them in water first to make them more pliable).

You do not need a perimeter frame round the trellis if it is being fixed to a wall, unless you want the look of a framed panel; the fixings will hold the lattice in formation. However, a free-standing trellis will need a frame unless it is well supported by fence posts or the framing members of a garden building. Remember that it may look strong surface is painted you will not be able to repaint it in the future unless you think about the problem now. The best solution is to position the bottom edge of the trellis panel 600mm (2ft) or so above ground level, and to hinge its lower edge to a wall-mounted batten. It will then be possible – with care – to release the other wall fixings and let the trellis fall away from the wall at an angle so you can paint behind it. The flexibility of the plant stems, allied to the generous ground clearance, should allow this movement of the support without damaging the plants themselves.

If you are mounting trellis on wooden supports, you can simply nail it in place. Use round wire nails with flat heads, rather than oval nails or panel pins, to provide a secure fixing that will resist the trellis pulling free under heavy wind loadings. Drill small pilot holes before driving in the nails, so you do not split the slim laths. Better still, use screws; they are more time-consuming to fix, but are more secure in the long run.

To mount trellis on a wall, it may be tempting to use masonry nails. Don't. They will be almost impossible to remove in the future if you want to replace the trellis. In any case, you want a gap between trellis and wall to allow

---

Below: Green painted trellis follows the line of this lower ground floor entrance. It adds style and privacy, whilst supporting flowering climbers.

plants to twine round it, and nails will pull it flat against the wall surface. Instead, use screws driven into wallplugs; again, drill pilot holes in the trellis first. When mounting the trellis, slip a short spacer cut from small-diameter copper or rigid plastic pipe over the screw before driving it into its wall plug. Use rust-proof screws wherever possible for all the fixings.

Fixing shallow trellis panels on top of a boarded fence is a popular way of gaining extra privacy once plants have become established. If you do this, stiffen the panels by adding a perimeter frame which can be secured to the top of the fence boards as well as to the posts themselves. Trellis panels do not, of course, have to be flat. Thanks to the flexibility of the laths, panels can be bent into gentle curves, allowing you to use them for making structures such as trellis arches and roofed walkways; you

TROMPE L'OEIL TRELLIS

There is no limit to the visual effects you can achieve with trellis...except your ingenuity. In the picture above, the rear wall of an already stunning loggia has been fitted with three panels of hand-made trelliswork to give the appearance of three apses framed by classical columns. The effect is almost perfect, thanks to the extremely skilful use of perspective in positioning the various converging and diverging lines.

A matching panel of traditional trellis fills in the garden side of the loggia, and even the roof support columns are constructed as tubes of trelliswork. The entire creation is finished with white microporous paint to minimise the need for future redecoration, a job even the most avid housepainter would approach with some trepidation.

could even construct a cylindrical arbour. The thinner the laths used and the larger the trellis grid, the more flexible the panel will be. However, do not expect to achieve a radius of curvature much smaller than about 500mm (20in) without splitting of the laths occurring.

Once your trellis is fixed in place, you can begin to train plants to climb it. As they spread, tuck the growing shoots in and out of the latticework so they get a good grip on the structure, and do not be afraid to add extra ties to the trellis at intervals to provide additional support – essential if you are growing fruit-bearing species, for example. As the plants spread, you can always add extra sections of trellis to support them; all you have to do is to match the existing trellis size and style when making up the new section.

FITTING TRELLIS TO A WALL

Installing a run of trellis along the top of a garden wall is a good way of gaining extra privacy as well as providing a support for climbing plants (1). Start by deciding on the length of post you require; this will be the height of the trellis plus about 600mm (2ft) to allow for fixing to the wall surface. Then cut the posts to length.

Hold each post against the wall, checking that it is vertical with a level, and mark the positions for two fixing screws in line with brick centres, not with the mortar joints. Then drill clearance holes in the posts.

Reposition the post against the wall and mark the positions of the clearance holes on the wall surface. Switch to a masonry drill bit and hammer action to drill the holes in the bricks, then insert wall plugs and screw the post into place. Next, offer up the first trellis panel to the

side of the post and drill clearance holes through its side frame members. Screw it to the post so it can act as a spacer for the next post.

Hold the second post in place against the other end of the panel, check that it is vertical and repeat the post fixing process (2). Then screw the trellis panel to the second post.

An alternative to driving screws into a previously-placed wallplug is to use a frame plug – a long wallplug complete with screw which you simply hammer in after drilling the post and wall holes (3).

With the second post in place, screw on the next section of trellis (4) and position and fix the next post. Continue in this way until the run is completed (5).

Above: *Open trelliswork and a simple arch form an attractive divider between the patio and the garden beyond.*

You can use trellis in a variety of ways to create a screen across the garden – perhaps to divide off a vegetable garden, to create a visual centrepiece, to hide an eyesore or gain extra privacy for when you are sitting out in the garden. You can incorporate an arch in the structure to form a walkway, either fitting a simple flat head or constructing a more elaborate curved design – the ideal support for climbing roses, for example. The screen can be left to weather naturally, or can be painted. White looks especially good against dark green foliage.

For a straight screen containing a central arch, set up one of the arch posts first (see pages 88-89 for details) to give you a point of reference from which to work. Then set up a stringline across the screen site to act as a guide to positioning the remaining posts (1).

Use a trellis panel as a spacer to gauge the required post separation, and install the other posts (2).

Stand the first panel up against the posts, resting its bottom edge on offcuts of wood so it stands squarely. Tap it sideways to line it up with the face of the post. Note that here the trellis is being fixed to the face of the posts instead of fitting between adjacent posts (3). Use this technique if you find that your post separation has altered while you were installing them and the panels no longer fit between them.

Nail the trellis to the top of the post. As a precaution against splitting the laths, drill pilot holes through the trellis before driving in the fixing nails.

Drive in another nail at the bottom of the post, and add intermediate fixings at roughly 300mm (12in) intervals.

Fit the other trellis panels in the same way, then nail an offcut of fence post across the top of the opening (4).

Finish the job by relaying any turf you lifted earlier, and add climbing plants along the foot of the screen.

DECKING, PATHS AND STEPS

SITTING-OUT AREAS, GARDEN PATHS AND STEPS DO NOT HAVE TO BE PAVED OR CONCRETED. WOOD MAKES AN UNUSUAL AND PRACTICAL ALTERNATIVE THAT SUITS ANY GARDEN, SINCE ITS COLOUR AND TEXTURE WILL BLEND IN NATURALLY WITH ITS SURROUNDINGS AS IT WEATHERS, AND THE SURFACE IS A SYMPATHETIC ONE TO WALK OR SIT ON. IT DRIES QUICKLY AFTER RAIN, AND WILL LAST FOR YEARS IF DURABLE TIMBER SPECIES ARE CHOSEN AND THE WOOD IS WELL TREATED WITH PRESERVATIVE BEFORE BEING PLACED IN POSITION. LASTLY, IT IS A FAR EASIER MATERIAL TO WORK WITH THAN CONCRETE OR STONE, ALTHOUGH RATHER MORE EXPENSIVE.

Above: *Baulks of heavy timber make a level sitting area in this attractively cobbled town garden.*

Right: *Carefully laid timber decking makes a stunning outdoor surface, especially when used on several levels.*

The first thing to think about is where you want your decking to go. The obvious site is at the back of the house, but you may prefer to site it elsewhere in the garden to take full advantage of the sun and the view or to gain greater privacy from your neighbours.

Next, examine the lie of the land. If it is basically level, you can build up your decking on bricks or low sleeper walls, aiming to keep the final surface of the deck about 150mm (6in) below the level of the damp proof course (dpc) in the house wall so that rain falling on the decking cannot splash back above the dpc and lead to damp penetration. If the land slopes, it is a simple matter to support the decking on posts, allowing you to create a level sitting area far more easily than with conventional building methods.

Thirdly, think about shape and size. Using timber gives you total flexibility as far as shape is concerned, while the size should take into account the likely use to which the decking will be put. Allow ample space round chairs and tables, both for access and to allow through traffic to cross the decking easily between house and garden.

Lastly, remember the safety angle. Decking more than about 450mm (18in) above the surrounding ground level should be fitted with handrails, and steps should be provided to link the decking to the garden. If you have small children, it is wise to have a balustrade with no more than 100mm (4in) gaps between the posts to stop heads getting trapped, and to design it so it is not readily climbable. A gate at the garden steps would then convert the decking into a full size outdoor playpen, perfect for toddlers. Gaps between the deck planking should be kept to no more than about 6mm (¼in), to allow easy surface drainage without letting chair legs slip into them.

CHOOSING MATERIALS

The obvious enemy of wood is rot, so the ideal types of timber to choose for a decking are rot resistant species such as Western red cedar or teak. However, the expense of these woods is likely to mean that most people will use ordinary softwood; this is fine so long as it is treated with preservative – ideally at the timber yard, using pressure or vacuum impregnation to ensure that the preservative penetrates deep into the wood.

Most of the structure can be built using sawn wood, with planed timber for the decking itself and for handrails and balustrades if these are required. The sizes needed will depend on the dimensions of the decking, and on whether it is built substantially above ground level or not. As a rough size guide, 100 x 50mm (4 x 2in) joists need

The decking in the picture above consists of a series of smaller modules laid side by side to cover the required area. Make them up by laying two bearers side by side and nailing slats across them with a slight gap between them for drainage (1). When the module reaches the desired length, trim off the bearers (2). Make steps up as shorter modules which can be skew-nailed into place on top of an unboarded section of a full-sized module (3).

Left: *Timber decking provides the perfect link between house and garden, and can be used for flights of steps too.*

supporting every 1.5m (5ft), while 150 x 50mm (6 x 2in) joists can span up to around 3m (10ft). Both are laid at 600mm (24in) centres, and are covered with 100 x 19mm or 150 x 19mm (4 x $^3/_4$in or 6 x $^3/_4$in) planks. Posts for supporting raised decking should be 100mm (4in) square, up to a maximum height of around 1.8m (6ft). For structures higher than this, professional advice should be sought to ensure that the components of the decking are correctly sited and are strong enough; the consequences of a collapse could be serious.

For low level decking, the joists can simply be set on individual bricks, garden walling blocks or paving slabs over an area of cleared vegetation, or can be placed directly on an existing area of concrete (see page 45). Low brick walls on concrete strip foundations will be needed if the ground clearance is to be more than a few inches. With raised platforms, the support posts will have to be set in concrete, or else must be bolted to fence spurs set in a concrete footing.

Most of the fixings can be made with galvanized nails, although coach bolts should be used to assemble the main framework with raised decks. You may need some masonry bolts if the decking adjoins the house and is to be suspended from a wall plate on the house wall. Lastly, have some wood preservative handy so you can treat all cut ends, joints and the like as you assemble the decking.

LOW LEVEL DECKING

If your decking will be just above existing ground level on a flat site, you can support the joists in several ways, as mentioned earlier. Mark out the position of the decking and clear the site of vegetation; then level and compact the surface. Set one corner brick or paver on a bed of sand, check that it is level and position other supports using this first one as a datum point. The sand bed makes it easy to bed the supports down to the required height. Space them to match the spans mentioned in the previous section.

Next, put a strip of roofing felt or dpc material on top of each support; a dab of bituminous mastic will help to keep it in place. Rest the joists on top of the supports, butt-joining lengths over the centre of each one if necessary, and then cover the ground beneath the decking with 2mm black polyethylene sheet and then weight it down with a 100-150mm (4-6in) layer of gravel to discourage weed growth.

Now you can start nailing or screwing on the decking planks to tie the whole structure together. Use a plywood offcut as a spacer to ensure an even gap between the planks. Remember that you do not have to lay the planks floorboard fashion; you can experiment with diagonal layouts and chevron patterns if you prefer.

At the edges of the decking, lay the boards so that their ends finish flush with the side joists; overhangs can be a trip hazard. If you wish, finish off the edges with a 50 x 25mm (2 x 1in) batten nailed in place level to the board ends, with the decking surface.

If you want to build a more substantial structure or need more ground clearance, build sleeper walls up to the required height in stretcher bond on concrete strip foundations 100mm (4in) thick. Space them to suit the joist dimensions, and incorporate a dpc in the wall two courses above ground level to keep the masonry dry.

With this type of construction built next to the house, it is often best to attach the house edge of the decking to the house wall; this saves having to build a sleeper wall here. You can do this in one of two ways. Either fix a timber wall plate to the wall with masonry bolts and skew nail the joists to this, or use galvanised steel joist hangers fixed to the wall to support the individual joist ends.

RAISED DECKING

Life becomes a little more complicated on steeply sloping sites, where the decking has to be supported by vertical posts. Start by marking out the site, indicating the positions of post holes with pegs. Then clear the site as before, and

Below: *Decking fixed wall-to-wall transforms this tiny back yard into an attractive outdoor living space.*

Above: *Heavy blocks of wood on a fine gravel base make a striking path.*

dig out the holes to a depth equal to one quarter of the post height and about 300mm (12in) across. Then set the posts in position (see pages 88-89) and concrete them in.

An alternative approach, suitable for decks up to about 1.2m (4ft) above ground level, is to set concrete fence spurs in the ground as described for wooden posts, and then to bolt the posts to the spurs. This avoids having timber buried in the ground where it may be attacked by rot.

Bolt the main cross bearers to the posts, checking that they are level as you attach them. Then trim off the post tops if necessary, and start screwing or bolting the joists to the cross bearers. Finally, fit the decking planks as before. With a raised deck of this sort, a guard rail is essential. Screw or bolt 50mm (2in) sq uprights to the joists all round the perimeter of the decking, and add handrails (and balusters if you wish). Then build up steps down to the garden or up to the house if the design calls for them. Make the treads at least 300mm (12in) deep from front to back, with a rise of no more than about 150mm (6in) per

step. Fit a handrail at each side if the flight has more than three steps.

SPLIT LEVEL DECKING

There is no reason why you should not have several areas of decking at different levels, and this can look particularly attractive on a sloping site. It will also make the construction easier, since you may be able to build several low level decks running into each other with steps between them instead of having to use posts to cope with the slope.

MAINTAINING DECKING

So long as the timber you used for your decking was preservative-treated, the only maintenance you will need to carry out will be an annual scrub-down in the spring to remove algae which will have grown during the winter, and regular inspections for splinters along board edges which could injure bare feet. Cut away any you find and sand the board edge smooth, giving it a slight chamfer to prevent further splitting.

If you want to spruce up the looks of your decking and maintain its defences against rot, brush on a generous coat of clear or pigmented preservative once every couple of years.

PATHS AND STEPS

There is no reason why you should not use timber to create paths and steps elsewhere in the garden too. Paths can be constructed in two ways; with planks or with roundels cut across the log and laid like small circular pavers. The former works only on virtually straight paths, while the latter can form either straight or curved paths with ease.

If you decide to use the plank method, use sawn timber with a fairly substantial cross section – say 150 x 50mm (6 x 2in) – and ensure that it has been pre-treated with preservative. Whether you lay the planks lengthwise, parallel with the path direction, or cross-wise depends on how the ground slopes.

If you prefer to use roundels, simply saw logs of various sizes into cylinders about 100mm (4in) long; anything shorter will split. A mixture of sizes not only makes an attractive path; you will also get a closer fit between adjacent roundels.

The best way of laying a planked path is to excavate the site to a depth of about 100mm (4in) and to put down a 50mm (2in) layer of fine gravel. This not only makes it easy to bed and level the

DECKING, PATHS AND STEPS

Left: Roundels set in concrete make an unusual surface for garden paths.

Below: Stout planks laid edge to edge allow the path to cope with gradients, and can even be built into steps (bottom).

planks; it also helps drain water away so they are not permanently water-logged. Then simply lay the planks in place, butting them together and securing the edge planks by driving in stout wooden pegs at regular intervals along the path perimeter.

Roundels really need setting in concrete to stop them working loose in use and becoming a trip hazard. Excavate to a depth of about 150mm this time, again put down a gravel bed and then tamp the roundels into position, butted together and levelled with their neighbours. Then fill the gaps between them with a dryish concrete mix to lock them all in position.

Use planks or roundels for making steps too, simply setting them in place to follow the slope of the ground. Mark out the position of the flight on the bank, and excavate step shapes in it. If you are using planks, again choose fairly substantial timber and cut the planks to the step width you require. Peg a vertical riser in place at the back of each step first, then lay the treads. Check that each plank is set level across its width and has a slight slope towards the front edge of the step, then secure the front plank of each step to the bank with long wooden pegs hammered into position.

If you are using roundels, you will have to cut the steps in the bank deep enough to accept units cut to a length of between 150 and 200mm (6 to 8in). Peg vertical planks in place first to form the front edge of each step, then place and concrete in the roundels that form the tread of the step.

GARDEN FURNITURE

GARDEN FURNITURE IS A FINE INVENTION, AND CAREFULLY CHOSEN PIECES CAN TRANSFORM YOUR PATIO OR GARDEN. GOOD-QUALITY ITEMS ARE EXPENSIVE TO BUY, BUT BY MAKING YOUR OWN YOU CAN SAVE MONEY AND CREATE FURNITURE THAT CAN STAY OUT COME RAIN OR SHINE, AND IF THEY ARE WELL BUILT IN THE FIRST PLACE THEY WILL NEED NO MAINTENANCE FOR MANY YEARS APART FROM AN OCCASIONAL WIPE OVER WHEN THE BIRDS HAVE BEEN EATING TOO MANY BERRIES. ABOVE ALL, BY CHOOSING DESIGNS AND MATERIALS CAREFULLY YOU CAN CREATE SEATING THAT LOOKS AS THOUGH IT BELONGS IN THE GARDEN INSTEAD OF JUST BEING PLANTED THERE.

Begin by thinking carefully about what you actually need. Is it simply a rustic bench where you can sit occasionally and admire the view? Or do you want furniture you can sunbathe on in comfort? If you will be eating out of doors, how many will you be catering for? Do you want individual seats or benches? What about an all-in-one picnic table-cum-bench? Do you need to provide shade? Answers to these questions will give you a basic shopping list – three sun loungers, a bench and two upright chairs, a table with an integral parasol and so on.

Next, think about how the furniture will be used. Working this out will help you define the *type* of furniture you want to make. For example, you may want to leave some items out all year round, so they will have to be durable and heavy enough not to blow away in high winds. Others will only be taken out when they are actually needed – typically items such as sunbeds and parasols. In between come things like upholstered seats and loungers, where just the cushions will be stored indoors when they are not in use. Think about this storage question now as well; if things are to be stored indoors, designing them to fold up means they will take up less space than 'solid' ones.

The last factor to consider is what the furniture will be made of, how well it will stand up to the elements and to everyday wear and tear, how easy it will be to carry about, and most importantly, how comfortable and practical it will be to use.

Wood's advantages are that it suits its environment, especially if left to weather naturally, and it wears well so long as a durable species is chosen or regular preservative treatment is applied. It is also warm to the touch and relatively easy to repair if damaged. Its drawbacks are that smaller items are light enough to be blown about in high winds, and larger ones tend to be heavy and decidedly non-portable. Wood also takes a while to dry out after rain. However, for traditional furniture in a traditional setting it is hard to beat.

Above: It takes little to make the simplest garden seat: just a baulk of timber set on two stout logs.

Left: Take a simple bench and paint it in a bold colour to create an eye-catching feature against the garden's foliage.

Ordinary softwood will soon deteriorate and begin to rot if used out of doors, so you must ensure that any wood you use is thoroughly impregnated with preservative – ideally by vacuum or pressure treatment carried out by your supplier. Some hardwoods require similar treatment, but there are several species that can be used out of doors without the need for extra protection. Some are softwoods, of which Western red cedar is the least expensive and most widely available. Others are hardwoods – either the tropical species from Africa, South America and Southeast Asia, or the temperate ones from areas such as Europe and North America.

From the first group of hardwoods comes teak – arguably the best wood of all for outdoor use. Its natural oiliness gives it more or less permanent resistance to moisture, and if it is left untreated it weathers to an attractive silvery grey colour. Other suitable tropical hardwoods include afrormosia, iroko and utile, but all are expensive.

American white or European oak is the best choice among temperate hardwoods. The Japanese and American red varieties are more prone to decay. Chestnut is a good runner up.

Man-made boards are of little use to the maker of outdoor furniture, with one exception: marine plywood. This is made from veneers that are either naturally weatherproof or have been treated with preservative, and the adhesive used to bond the veneers together is waterproof too. Avoid other grades even if labelled as suitable for exterior use; the adhesive may be up to the job, but the veneers are not unless completely protected from the weather by paint or

varnish. In any case, plywood seldom blends in well in the garden because it is man-made; natural timber simply looks more natural.

It is important to think about how you will assemble your garden furniture. The trouble with nails and screws is that steel rusts. Worse still, being out of doors the wood will swell and shrink as the seasons change, and this will put considerable strain on any fixings you use. The best solution is to rely on simple but sturdy woodworking joints – mainly variations on the mortise and tenon joint, with the occasional halving joint used where necessary. Tenons can then be locked in place with pegs or wedges so that the joint stays tight even without the use of adhesive. The best framing joint of all is the projecting wedged tenon (also known as the tusk tenon), where the projecting end of the tenon is itself mortised to accept a tapered wedge which can simply be driven in a little further whenever the joint shows any sign of movement.

Garden Furniture

Adhesives are generally of little use for assembling garden furniture; only the urea-formaldehyde (UF) and epoxy types are totally weatherproof. Unfortunately the oiliness that protects the best outdoor timbers such as teak from the weather also stops water-based UF adhesive from bonding well. Interlocking joints really are the best solution for outdoor furniture.

The way you design your furniture has a bearing on how well it performs too. For example, avoid wide pieces which will shrink and swell proportionately more than narrow ones. In addition, their exposed surfaces will tend to cup curl up at the edges on the side furthest from the centre of the tree from which they were cut. Narrow pieces also help to shed rainwater more easily, which is why slatted designs are so widely used for seats and table tops.

Endgrain will absorb moisture much more readily than side grain, so try to design your furniture so that as much endgrain as possible is concealed. Where it is exposed, seal it with a thin solution of UF adhesive, bevel or round off the end of the component so water runs off it easily, or cap it otherwise.

Lastly, remember that garden furniture often has to stand on uneven ground, so pieces should be designed to stand on legs or feet rather than on the edges of boards. Remember that furniture with three legs is the perfect solution: it never wobbles!

Above: A table built round a specimen tree makes an unusual garden centre-piece with its own built-in shade.

Left: If garden furniture is made from a durable species, it can be left to weather naturally to an attractive silvery grey colour.

Below: Restrict the use of paint to furniture that is normally kept indoors.

MAKING A SLATTED TABLE

This table incorporates all the principles mentioned earlier. It is made from Western red cedar; however, the cross-sectional sizes given correspond to the usual finished dimensions of other softwoods which may be more readily available than cedar.

The long rails which support the slats are bridle-jointed to the tops of the legs, while the cross rails are pegged into mortises. The slats are, with two exceptions, secured by screws driven up from beneath the table, and are positioned so they conceal and protect the vulnerable end grain on the tops of the legs. The ends of the long rails have optional curved detailing, while the taper and groove at the foot of each leg is also an option; they can be left plain and square if this is preferred.

Start by cutting the four legs overlong; their final length will be 725mm (28in). Then mark the open mortises for the bridle joints as shown in (1) overleaf. They should be about 40mm (1½in) wide and 10mm (³⁄₈in) shorter than the width of the long rail, which is cut from 75 x 50mm (3 x 2in) wood. Cut them out with a tenon saw and coping saw.

Mark the mortises for the cross rails on the inner face of each leg (1 overleaf) and chisel them out to a depth of about 50mm (2in) ready to accept the tenoned ends of the cross-rails. This minimises the exposure of their end grain.

Now mark the bridles on the long rails, starting with the shoulder on the under side which should be kept shallow to preserve the strength of the rail while providing a positive lock to the leg when the joint is assembled. Then mark the shoulders on the rail's thickness with your marking gauge so its reduced width matches the size of the bridles on the top of the legs. Remove the waste wood with a fine tenon saw and broad chisel (2). Finish the rails by marking and cutting the decorative end curves if required.

Use the shoulders cut on the long rails as a guide to marking the tenon positions on the cross rails, then use a marking gauge to set the tenon width so it matches that of the mortise in the legs. Cut the tenons, leaving a 10mm (³⁄₈in) shoulder on the underside.

Cut the tapers on the legs at this stage if you want them, using a tenon saw, and add the grooves on their inner faces with a carving gouge or a router (3).

Drill right through each leg where the centre of the cross-rail tenon will be, using a bit to match the size of your pegging dowel. Push the tenon in and use the bit again to mark the hole position on it. Remove the tenon and make another mark 1.5mm (¹⁄₁₆in) closer to the shoulder than the one made by the bit. Drill through the tenon at this second mark, and reinsert it in its mortise.

Taper the end of a length of dowel and hammer it home right through the joint. It will automatically pull the joint

tight. Trim and plane the ends of the dowel off flush with the leg. Repeat the process for the other three joints to complete the two H-shaped leg assemblies. If you are using softwood other than cedar, apply a liberal coat of clear wood preservative to all exposed areas of end-grain.

Drop the long rails into their bridles on top of the legs to assemble the table frame. Leave these joints unglued so the table top can be easily removed for storage; so long as you cut the bridle joints carefully earlier, they should be a perfect fit – tight enough to lock the whole structure rigidly togther, yet easy to knock apart with a mallet if you want to dismantle the table for storage. Then glue the 25mm (1in) square battens through which the slats will be screwed to the inner faces of the long rails. Note that you must fit one long length of batten between the legs and a short length to the inner face of the projecting ends of each rail.

Loose-lay the slats on the frame, with the centre one over a carefully-marked centre line. Space them out so that the middle slat of each group of five to the left and right of the centre slat fits precisely over the top of the legs. Mark the slat positions on the rails; they

Below: *This garden table and bench are made from Western red cedar. The unusual curve in the seat slats gives the set an oriental feel.*

should end up about 15mm (⁵/₈in) apart. Drill clearance holes through the 25mm (1in) square batten in line with the slat centres, and counter sink them on the underside.

Cut the centre slat to length, saw both ends to a double 60° splay, and drive its brass fixing screws up through the holes drilled in the batten and into the underside of the slat. Check the

length of screw you use to ensure that it penetrates the slat as far as possible without its point breaking through the slat surface.

Cut a single 60° splay on one end of the next slat, but leave the other end over-long. Lay it in position, with spacers to keep the correct separation between it and the centre batten, and align the splayed ends using an offcut of

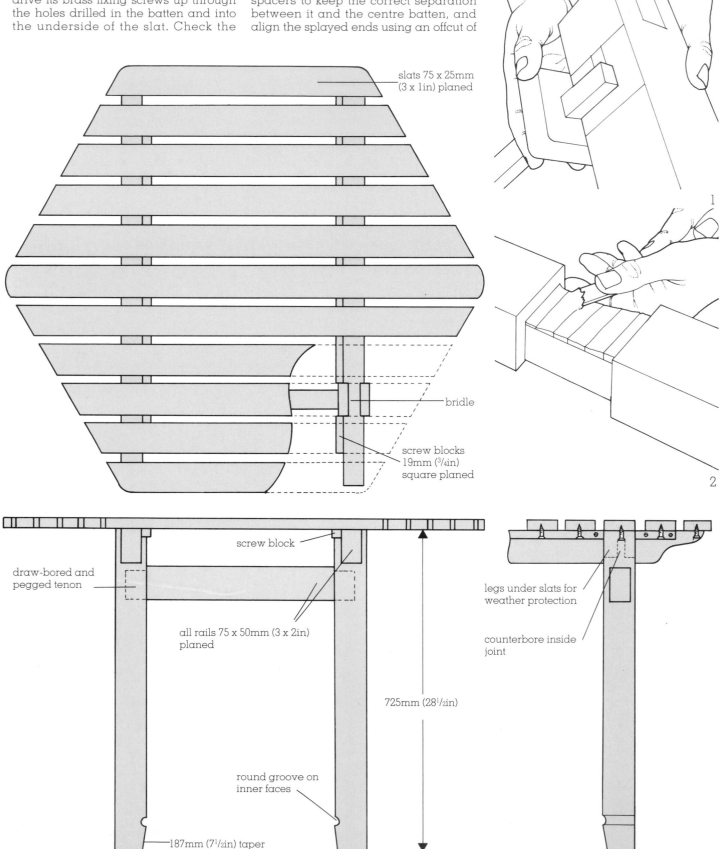

slats 75 x 25mm (3 x 1in) planed

bridle

screw blocks 19mm (³/₄in) square planed

1

2

screw block

draw-bored and pegged tenon

all rails 75 x 50mm (3 x 2in) planed

legs under slats for weather protection

counterbore inside joint

725mm (28¹/₂in)

round groove on inner faces

187mm (7¹/₂in) taper

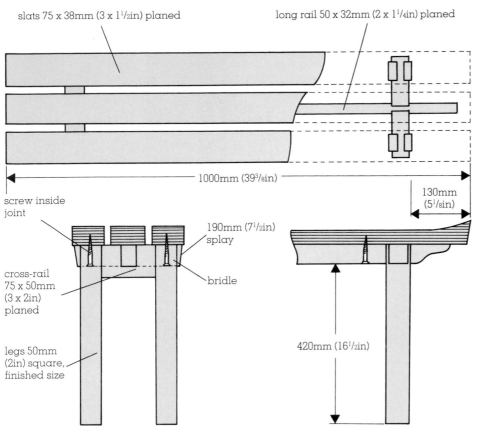

slats 75 x 38mm (3 x 1½in) planed

long rail 50 x 32mm (2 x 1¼in) planed

1000mm (39⅜in)

130mm (5⅛in)

screw inside joint

190mm (7½in) splay

cross-rail 75 x 50mm (3 x 2in) planed

bridle

legs 50mm (2in) square, finished size

420mm (16½in)

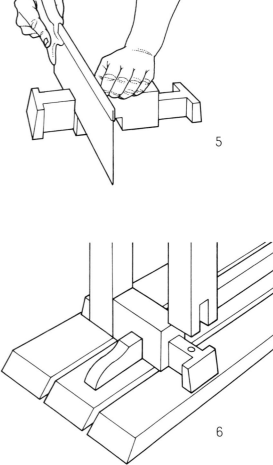

5

6

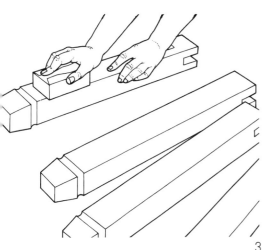

3

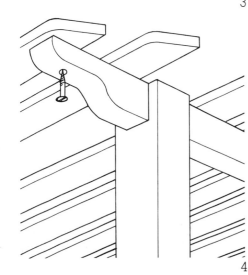

4

wood held against them. Then use a sliding bevel to mark the position of the splay on the other end of the slat, cut it to length and screw the slat in place. Repeat this process to cut and fit the other slats, with the exception of the two that will cover the tops of the legs. Note too that the outermost slats are fixed by driving screws up through holes drilled in the ends of the long rails (4).

Lift the table top off, turn it upside down and drill counterbores and clearance holes in the undersides of the bridles in the long rails. Position the two missing slats carefully and drive screws through the counterbores into their undersides to secure them to the rails. Replace the table top to complete the assembly.

Finish off the table by treating all exposed surfaces either with teak oil or with a clear wood preservative. Rub oil in with a rag, wiping off any excess after leaving it to soak in for a while. Brush preservative on, flooding end grain thoroughly for maximum protection.

Making a matching bench

The slatted bench consists of four legs, two short cross rails that link each pair together, and a long centre rail that links the two cross-rails. Set out the joints for both cross-rails on one piece of wood for ease of handling, with the open mortises for the long rail centred on the upper edge of the piece between the two pairs

of bridle joints (5). Then cut the joints and separate the two rails, which slot into matching open mortises cut in the tops of the legs.

Flare the ends of the slats by driving wedges into three parallel saw cuts, or shape them from solid timber, then attach them to the leg assembly. Fix the two outer slats with screws driven up through the bridle joints (6), and attach the centre one via a counterbore in the underside of the centre rail. Finish it like the table.

Siting seats

The final step is to decide where you want to sit. You may be lucky enough to enjoy a magnificent view from a particular spot in the garden – a perfect choice. On the other hand, the view may be not worth looking at, so you should look for a site that lets you enjoy individual features of your own garden – a pool, rockery or specimen tree, for example. Try to find a site that is in the sun as much as possible (unless you prefer to sit in the shade, of course), and is also well sheltered from the prevailing winds on breezy days.

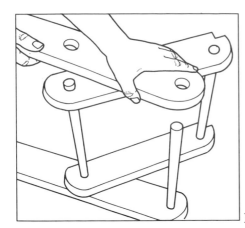

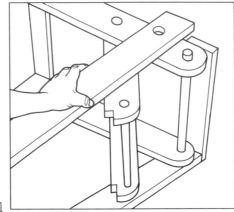

1

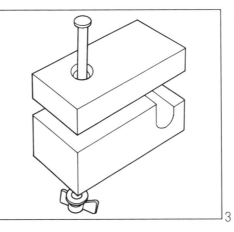

2

FOLDAWAY FURNITURE

The attractive slatted-top table and its matching benches have one major advantage over most other items of garden furniture; the table can be folded flat for ease of transportation and storage, yet can be set up quickly wherever you want it. It is extremely simple to make, since only butt joints (glued and nailed or screwed together) are used in its construction. The table is made mainly from 100 x 25mm (4 x 1in) wood, while the matching benches use 75 x 25mm (3 x 1in) wood throughout. Full details of all the parts you will need are given in the cutting list below.

CUTTING LIST

The table

From 100 x 25mm (4 x 1in) wood cut:
15 top slats 750mm (29$^{1}/_{2}$in) long
2 side rails 1495mm (58$^{7}/_{8}$in) long
2 top end rails 706mm (27$^{3}/_{4}$in) long
2 bottom end rails 704mm (27$^{3}/_{4}$in) long
4 legs 765mm (30$^{7}/_{8}$in) long
4 leg braces 456mm (18in) long

From 25mm (1in) diameter dowel cut
2 top leg bars 750mm (29$^{1}/_{2}$in) long
2 brace bars 704mm (27$^{3}/_{4}$in) long
2 brace bars 658mm (26in) long

In addition you will need
2 125mm (5in) lengths of 75 x 50mm
  (3 x 2in) wood and
2 125mm (5in) lengths 75 x 38mm
  (2 x 1$^{1}/_{2}$in) wood for the leg clamps
2 100mm (4in) long coach bolts 6mm
  ($^{1}/_{4}$in) in diameter, plus matching wing
  nuts and washers
8 50mm (2in) No 8 rustproof counter-
  sunk woodscrews

The bench

From 75 x 25mm (3 x 1in) wood cut:
15 top slats 400mm (15$^{3}/_{4}$in) long
2 side rails 1195mm (47in) long
2 top end rails 356mm (14in) long
2 bottom end rails 400mm (15$^{3}/_{4}$in) long
4 legs 702mm (27$^{5}/_{8}$in) long
4 leg braces 410mm (16$^{1}/_{8}$in) long

3

For both pieces you will need 19mm ($^{3}/_{4}$in) and 38mm (1$^{1}/_{2}$in) rustproof (sherardized) oval wire nails, some waterproof urea formaldehyde (UF) wood glue and some clear or pigmented wood preservative.

Start by marking out and cutting all the components to length, with the exception of the table legs and leg braces which should be cut slightly overlong so their ends can be rounded off driving assembly.

Clamp the table side rails together and drill a 25mm (1in) diameter hole through each end of both rails, 71mm (2$^{3}/_{4}$in) from their ends.

Draw a centre line along one face of each leg and mark off along it at 48, 53 and 268mm (1$^{7}/_{8}$, 2$^{1}/_{8}$in and 10$^{1}/_{2}$in) intervals. Set a compass point on the 53mm (2$^{1}/_{8}$in) mark and scribe an arc from one edge of the leg to the other to draw the shape of the top of the leg. Measure 715mm (18$^{1}/_{8}$in) along the centre line from the top of the arc and square a line across the leg. This is the bottom of the leg. Measure back 50mm (2in) from this line and square a second line across the leg. Stand the end of an offcut of 100 x 25mm (4 x 1in) wood on the face of the leg so one narrow edge is aligned with this second line and draw round it to mark the cut out for the bottom end rails. Mark out the other three legs identically, then cut them to length, round off their tops with a coping saw or jig saw, remove the marked cut outs and drill

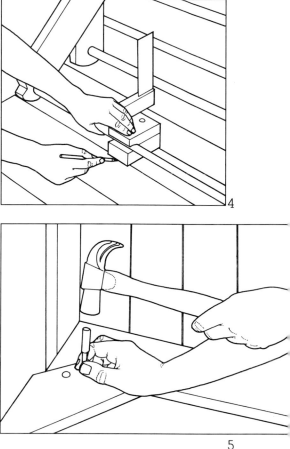

4

5

25mm (1in) diameter holes through each leg at the 48 and 268mm (1$\frac{7}{8}$ and 10$\frac{1}{2}$in) marks made earlier.

To make up the folding leg braces, first cut the four 456mm (18in) long pieces that form their sides, mark a centre line along each one and make a mark on this 53mm (2$\frac{1}{8}$in) from one end. Draw an arc and round off one end of each brace. Make a second mark on the centre line, 311mm (12$\frac{1}{4}$in) from the first mark, and draw a similar arc here, then round off this end too and drill 25mm (1in) diameter holes through the braces at both marks. Finally use a tenon saw to cut a 35 x 22mm (1$\frac{3}{8}$ x $\frac{7}{8}$in) notch in one end of each brace; this fits round the table's bottom end rail when the legs are folded.

To assemble the table, glue together the leg braces first, checking that the longer bar protrudes by an equal amount at each side. Then slot these protruding ends into the holes in two of the table legs (1), check that they swivel freely and link the two legs with a bottom end rail (glued and nailed in place) and a top leg bar (glued), again checking that the latter protrudes by the same amount through each leg. Repeat the process to assemble the other end of the table, then link the two end frames with the two long side rails and the top end rails after checking that the leg rotates freely (2), and complete the assembly by nailing and gluing on the top slats.

Garden Furniture

Make up the clamps as shown (3). Fit the bolt through the thinner block, then fit the clamp round the leg bar using the washer and wing nut (4). With the leg at 90° to the table top, mark the block position on the underside of the table. Undo the clamp and screw the thinner block to the underside of the table top. The clamp will then secure the leg in both the open and closed positions.

To assemble the bench, link the side and top end rails first, then add the slats before attaching the legs, the bottom end rails and finally the angled braces (5). Finish both pieces with a generous coat of wood preservative.

Making a patio set

This colourful set of patio furniture could not be easier to make. The table top and bench seats are simply planks of wood, set on sturdy X-frame legs to form a solid structure that is heavy enough to stay put even in high winds. They are finished in microporous paint, which allows water vapour to pass through the paint film without causing the inevitable cracking and peeling that occurs with ordinary paints. This type weathers by erosion, so redecorating is simply a case of washing down the existing paintwork and applying a fresh coat over the top.

Make up the table top first, to whatever size you need for your patio. The table illustrated has a top consisting of eight pieces of 150 x 38mm (6 x 1½in) wood, screwed to two 50 x 38mm (2 x 1½in) transverse bearers with a narrow gap between each plank to allow rainwater to drain off easily. Countersink the screw holes deeply and fill the recesses with exterior-quality wood filler to remove any risk of rust showing through the paint finish. Make up the bench seats in exactly the same way.

Next, make up the legs from two pieces of 100 x 38mm (4 x 1½in) wood, joined with a cross-halving joint at an angle of 60°. If you do not have a protractor and a sliding bevel to help you set out the angles, remember that all three sides of a triangle with 60° corner angles measure the same length, and use this to set the pieces at the correct angle. Cut the halving joints with a tenon saw and chisel, check their fit, then drill through the joint and secure it with a coach bolt.

Screw each leg assembly to the outer face of a transverse bearer beneath the table top or seat. Then screw a short length of 50 x 38mm (2 x 1½in) wood to the under-side of the top/seats, at right angles to each bearer, to which the diagonal leg braces will be attached. Measure up the required length for each pair of braces, cut their ends at 45° angles, drill deep counterbores for the fixing screws and fix them in position. Finally, sand and paint each item.

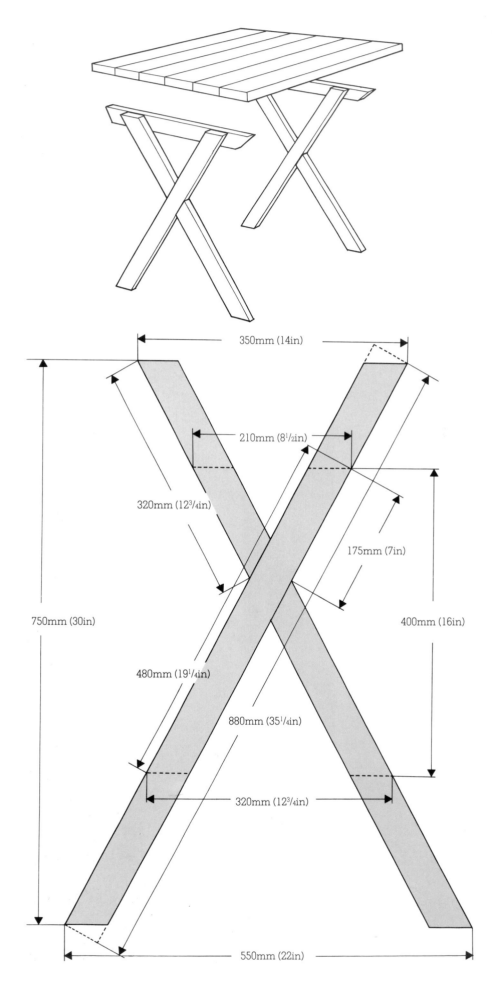

350mm (14in)

210mm (8½in)

320mm (12¾in)

175mm (7in)

750mm (30in)

400mm (16in)

480mm (19¼in)

880mm (35¼in)

320mm (12¾in)

550mm (22in)

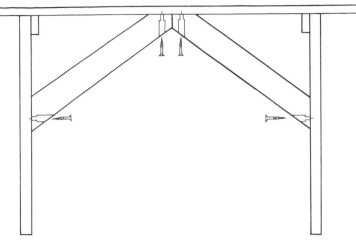

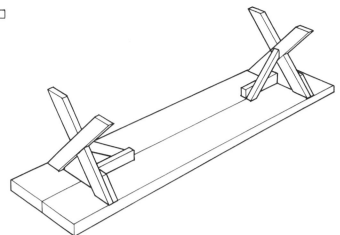

Below: Clever use of colour gives this
furniture, deck and rails great impact.

GARDEN BUILDINGS

THE FEATURES THAT ARE LIKELY TO MAKE THE BIGGEST VISUAL IMPACT ON YOUR GARDEN ARE ANY BUILDINGS YOU CHOOSE TO PUT IN IT, SIMPLY BY VIRTUE OF THEIR LIKELY SIZE. MOST GARDENS BOAST A SHED OF ONE SORT OR ANOTHER, USUALLY UNTIDILY FULL OF GARDENING TOOLS, MATERIALS AND BROKEN DECKCHAIRS, BUT SUCH A FUNC-TIONAL BUILDING IS RARELY A VISUAL DELIGHT AND USUALLY ENDS UP HIDDEN AT THE BOTTOM OF THE GARDEN. MORE EYECATCHING ARE BUILDINGS CONSTRUCTED FOR LEISURE USE, SUCH AS A GAZEBO OR SUMMERHOUSE.

Garden buildings have a long and fasci-nating history. Ever since man has culti-vated his garden as a thing of beauty rather than a source of food, he has graced it with buildings of one sort or another. Some were included as part of the overall design, perhaps providing a visual centrepiece to the scheme of things as well as offering a pleasant place to sit and admire the garden layout. Many were built as follies – architectural jokes and oddities with a certain curiosity value.

Below: *A well-kept summerhouse in the style of a Swiss chalet makes an attrac-tive feature in any garden.*

Left: *Open trelliswork can be used to good effect to make a garden arbour, and blends in well with the greenery if left to weather naturally. This one has apparently turned into a fern house.*

Below: *Trellis walls and a shingle covered roof turn this miniature bandstand into an eye catching garden building that is also a shady retreat.*

Other buildings were sited to take advantage of a view, either of the surrounding scenery or of the house itself – the belvedere or gazebo. The storage shed, on the other hand, is really a necessary but visually uninspiring garden feature unless it is carefully designed and sited and is kept in good condition. Few are.

The manufacturers of sectional garden buildings offer a comprehensive range of prefabricated summerhouses, sheds and greenhouses, and if you can wield a spanner and a screwdriver you can build one in an afternoon. However, you will be stuck with the maker's design, shape and size, and unless you are happy with that you will have far greater flexibility if you design and construct your own garden buildings.

There are several factors you need to take into account if you decide to take this route. The first is the raw material you will use. This is likely to be softwood, on grounds of cost as much as anything else, and it is essential to buy wood that has been pre-treated with preservative.

The second is the type of roof and roof covering you want. As far as roof type is concerned, your choice lies between having a ridged roof or a flat one (in fact, usually sloping at between 5° and 10°). Ridged roofs always look more attractive, even if they are a little more

difficult to construct. As far as roof coverings are concerned, you must first decide whether the structure is to be weatherproof or not. Most prefabricated garden buildings have a boarded roof covered with roofing felt, and although this is really your only choice for a flat roof it never blends in very well with the garden. Better choices for ridged roofs are wooden shingles or, if the building is substantial enough, small clay tiles. If the roof is decorative rather than functional, you can use open slats or trellis and then train plants over it if you wish.

The third factor to consider is the wall finish, and here too what you choose depends on whether or not the structure must be weatherproof. If it must, timber cladding or shingles are the obvious choice. If not, then you can again use trellis....or simply leave the structure with open sides.

Lastly, does the building need a floor, or will it simply stand directly on a concrete or paved base? If you decide to have a floor, you need to make some provision for keeping rising damp from rotting it away by setting it clear of the ground or placing a damp proofing layer underneath it. Strips of roofing felt laid beneath the floor joists are one solution to the problem.

When you have made these choices about the building's function, you can

turn your mind to its design. You can borrow your inspiration from prefabricated buildings, from magazine illustrations, even from history books if you want a miniature Parthenon down the garden. If the building is to be open to the elements you have a virtually free hand, but summerhouses and garden sheds are likely to draw on at least some prefabricated components such as doors and windows, and the styles and sizes available will have some bearing on the final design of the building.

Think too about the building's decorative finish, especially as far as ease of future maintenance is concerned. Avoid traditional paint and varnish, which will eventually crack and flake; go instead for microporous paints or wood stains (both easy to re-coat when necessary) if you want colour, and use clear wood preservative if you prefer a natural finish. Lastly, think about security for summerhouses and storage sheds. They often contain valuable tools and furniture, and so should be securely locked.

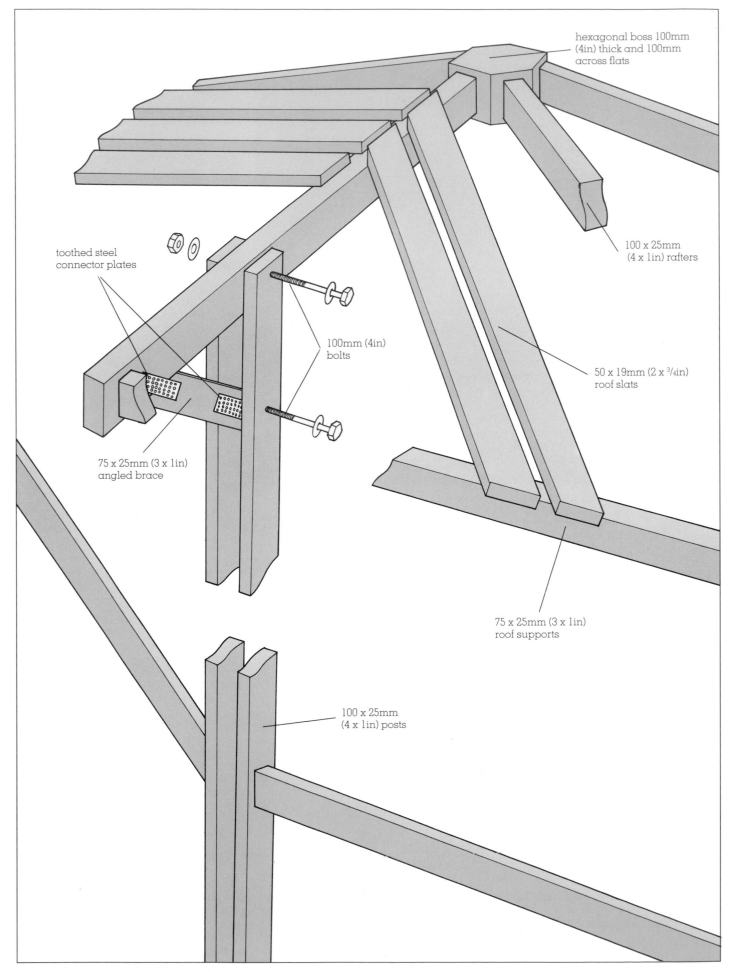

hexagonal boss 100mm
(4in) thick and 100mm
across flats

100 x 25mm
(4 x 1in) rafters

toothed steel
connector plates

100mm (4in)
bolts

50 x 19mm (2 x ³/₄in)
roof slats

75 x 25mm (3 x 1in)
angled brace

75 x 25mm (3 x 1in)
roof supports

100 x 25mm
(4 x 1in) posts

MAKING AN OPEN GAZEBO

This unusual hexagonal building provides an attractive centrepiece for any garden, with its open sides and slatted roof offering the prospect of pleasantly cool shade within. Its main frame consists of six pairs of uprights linked on five sides by rails at waist height. Each pair of posts sandwiches a rafter and an angled support brace, and the projecting ends of the rafters are linked by perimeter roof support members. Each roof panel has two further roof supports, fixed parallel to the perimeter ones at intervals equal to one-third and two-thirds of the rafter length respectively. The rafters meet at the apex of the roof, which consists of a hexagonal centre boss, and each of the six roof panels is covered with spaced battens cut and fixed so that adjacent pairs of roof slopes have an attractive chevron pattern.

The posts and rafters are all cut from 100 x 25mm (4 x 1in) wood. The roof supports and angled braces are 75 x 25mm (3 x 1in) wood, and the roof slats are 50 x 19mm (2 x ³⁄₄in) in size, spaced about 25mm (1in) apart. The hexagonal central roof boss is cut out of a block of wood 100mm (4in) thick and is about 100mm (4in) wide, measured across opposite 'flats'. Glue two pieces of 100 x 50mm (4 x 2in) wood together to make it if you cannot easily obtain wood 100mm (4in) thick.

Above right: *The open slatted roof of this unusual hexagonal arbour has a carefully matched chevron pattern on each of the roof sections.*

Below: *The roof provides varying amounts of shade as the sun moves.*

Start by marking out the site accurately. Since a hexagon consists of six adjacent triangles, each with a 60° angle at each corner, the simplest way of setting the post positions is to start at the centre of the structure. Set up a string line passing through this point, and measure along it in each direction out from the centre a distance X equal to half the overall width of the building to mark the positions of one pair of opposite posts.

Next, take one string line of length X from the centre point and one of the same length from one post position. where they meet is the next post position. Repeat this exercise all the way round to position the six sets of posts.

Build the structure by making up the six post/brace/rafter assemblies first, using bolts and steel connecting plates as shown in the drawing. Then, with the aid of a helper, erect opposite pairs in turn, screwing them to the centre boss with pre-drilled metal strips. Brace them all in position while the concrete sets round the posts, then add the rails and roof supports. Finally cut the roof slats and nail them in place.

Making a lean-to

SHELTER

This striking garden shelter would be an attractive and practical addition to any garden, and can be built up against a perimeter wall or fence, or against the house itself. It is also extremely simple to construct. The four corner posts are set in concrete to provide a solid framework for the building, and an additional post in the middle of the back wall provides extra support for the waney-edged timber cladding which helps give the building its rustic appearance. The roof is supported on two sturdy bearers that

link the corner posts at the front and back; these are bridged by rafters secured at their top and bottom ends by birdsmouth joints at 600mm (2ft) centres.

Tiling battens run across the rafters, and are spaced to match the size of the second-hand clay tiles used for the roof. Any ordinary roof tiles can be used; you may want to match the roof of the house, especially if the building is against the house wall. Second-hand tiles, if you can find them, help give the building a 'ready aged' look.

To prevent any risk of high winds lifting the topmost row of tiles, lead flashing is secured to the top of the rear wall and is dressed down over the ridge and onto the face of the tiles.

Above: *Naturally weathered timber and old second-hand tiles combine to create a garden shelter with a rustic look.*

With the main frame erected and the roof structure in place, the cladding and trellis panels are fixed in position to battens which are themselves nailed to the inner faces of the corner posts. The finishing touches are provided by adding a fascia board (which could be given a decorative edging) and making the two curved brackets that fill in the front corners of the open structure. These are made by gluing two pieces of 100mm (4in) square timber together with waterproof urea-formaldehyde adhe-

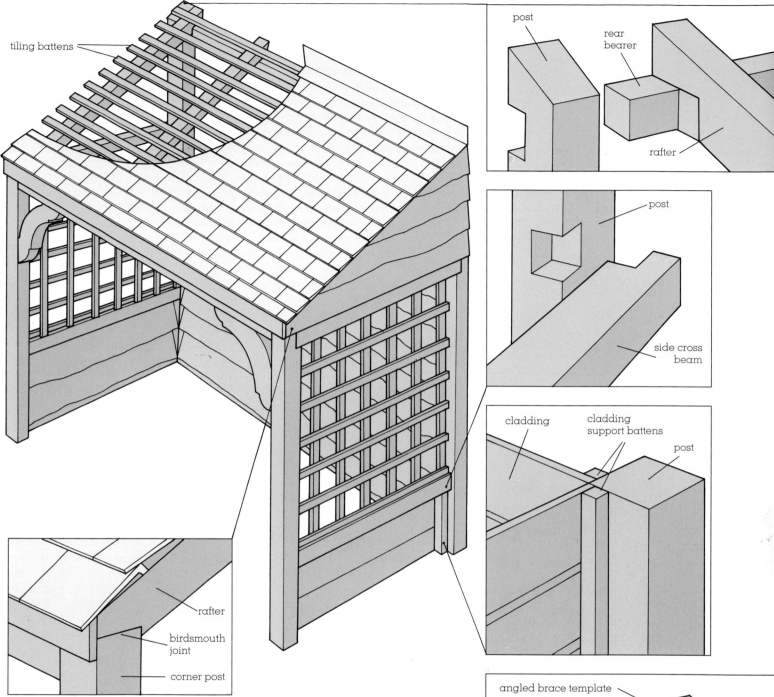

tiling battens

post
rear bearer
rafter

post
side cross beam

cladding
cladding support battens
post

rafter
birdsmouth joint
corner post

angled brace template
100mm (4in) square wood blocks

sive, and then marking out the bracket shape on the block, ready for cutting and fitting.

Finish the building with a generous coat or two of preservative stain.

You can tailor the size of the shelter to suit the space available in your garden. This building is about 3.6m (12ft) wide and 1.5m (5ft) deep from front to back, but you can vary both width and depth as necessary. The overall height is about 2.75m (9ft) at the ridge and 2m (6ft 6in) at the eaves. If you do alter the building's dimensions, aim to keep the roof slope the same as here – a gradient of about 1 in 2.

Cut the posts slightly over-long and set them in place, then mark their

heights and cut them to length with their tops angled to match the roof slope. Next, mark out and cut the recesses in the posts to accept the ends of the main cross-bearers. and nail these in place.

Add the rafters at 600mm (2ft) centres, with the outermost pair set against the sides of the corner posts. Cut birdsmouth joints in each rafter so it sits neatly over the bearers at the top and bottom of the roof slope. Fix the tiling battens at spacings to suit the tiles you are using.

Add the side cross beams and the battens to support the cladding and trellis. Then fit the lead flashing, add the fascia board and make and fit the decorative corner brackets.

Above: *The details to the main drawing show how the various frame members fit together, how the tiling and cladding are fixed and how the angled braces are marked out for cutting to shape.*

OTHER GARDEN BUILDINGS

Unless you are fortunate enough to have a garage large enough to provide storage space as well as room for the car, you are sure to need a garden shed of some description in which to keep your lawnmower, your other gardening tools, bags of fertiliser, bottles of weedkiller and all the other paraphernalia the average gardener always collects. Such a building might do double duty as a workshop or potting shed, and could also store foldaway garden furniture and even things like a mobile barbecue. Think carefully about exactly what you will expect it to cope with before deciding on how big a shed you will need. If in doubt, add a metre (3ft) to the length and width you first thought of; you will soon fill up the additional space.

As with other garden buildings, you have the choice between buying something prefabricated or building it yourself. With the cost of wood being relatively high nowadays, you will have difficulty matching the cost of a prefabri-

cated shed if you decide on the do-it-yourself route, but you will at least be able to design and construct a building that precisely matches your requirements. You will also be able to pay more attention to its looks; most prefabricated sheds do tend to have a somewhat utilitarian appearance.

Unlike other garden buildings, a shed really needs a floor. Without one, its contents will be permanently damp: tools will rust and dry materials such as fertiliser will rapidly turn into a useless solid lump. A simple boarded floor on preservative treated battens is all that is required; set the battens on strips of roofing felt or similar material, laid on the concrete base under the building, to keep the floor dry.

Incorporate windows only if you intend to use the building as a workshop. Would-be burglars are likely to find a selection of useful housebreaking tools in a shed, and can easily break a

Below: *A garden shed need not be hidden at the bottom of the garden if it is well designed and well maintained.*

window to gain access, especially if the shed is sited away from the house. If you do need windows, consider fitting them with wired glass or, better still, a plastic glazing material such as polycarbonate sheeting which is almost unbreakable. Make sure that the door is secure too, ideally with a padlocked hasp and staple at the top and bottom of the door in addition to any existing lock or latch. Even if you are not the target of a housebreaker, there is a busy trade these days in expensive garden equipment such as lawnmowers. It is well worth keeping yours securely under lock and key.

If you plan to use the shed as a workshop, especially in the winter months, it pays to insulate it. Cover the floor with 25mm (1in) thick rigid polystyrene board and lay tongued-and-grooved boards over it to form a floating floor. Cut pieces of the same insulating board to fit between the wall framing timbers, then line the walls with oil tempered hardboard (more damp-resistant than the ordinary grade) or thin plywood. Use the same technique to insulate the underside of the roof too. You could even double-glaze the window and draughtstrip the door.

Lastly, you will find an electricity supply invaluable, both for supplying light and power to the workshop and also for powering electrical equipment such as hedgetrimmers. Make sure that the circuit complies with local wiring regulations.

Above: *The traditional potting shed, with its wall to wall windows facing the sun, is the perfect retreat for the gardener who likes to raise everything from seed or from carefully potted cuttings.*

Left: *Timber cladding is the perfect wall surface for all sorts of garden buildings, especially when the wood is left to weather naturally.*

GAZEBOS

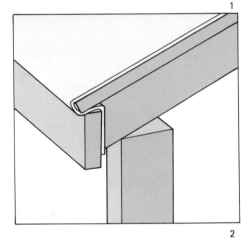

BUILDING A TIMBER SHED

If you decide to construct a garden shed from scratch, you have the opportunity to use good-quality materials and a high standard of joinery to produce a building that will last for years, especially if you make sure that all the wood you use has been pre-treated with preservative.

Begin by making up the floor, using 75 x 50mm (3 x 2in) joists set at about 300mm (12in) centres for extra rigidity. Notch the joist ends to accept 50 x 25mm (2 x 1in) cross battens that will keep the joists square while you add the floor decking. This can be tongued-and-grooved boards, plywood or roofing-grade chipboard, nailed to the joists. Set the completed frame in place on its base, with strips of roofing felt under the joists to keep the damp at bay.

Next, make up the four wall panels to the required dimensions, again using 75 x 50mm (3 x 2in) timber with vertical studs at about 450mm (18in) centres and a horizontal rail halfway up each panel for extra strength. All the joints are simple halving joints, glued and screwed together. Position door and window frame members to suit the sizes of the off-the-shelf door and window. The end walls have integral gables, with the angled rafters notched into tops of the wall studs.

When the wall frames are complete, stand two adjacent frames in position on the edge of the floor and cramp them together. Drill two holes right through both the corner posts, about one-third and two-thirds of the way up, then bolt the two frames together with carriage bolts. Repeat the process with the other panels to complete the shed frame (1).

Next, fix the remaining rafters, which are simply nailed to the tops of the side

wall frames, and start attaching the wall cladding. Cover the end walls first, working from the bottom upwards and cutting the pieces so they finish flush with the face of the side wall frames. Clad these next, letting the cladding overlap the cut ends of the cladding on the end walls to protect its vulnerable end grain from water penetration. Treat the end grain of the side wall cladding with preservative once it is in position.

You can now turn your attention to the roof. Cut and fit two panels of exterior-grade plywood or chipboard, screwing each panel to the rafters at 300mm (12in) intervals (2). Lay the first strip of roofing felt in position, taking it over the ridge of the roof if it is wide enough, and fix it with galvanised clout nails. Lay the second strip on the other side of the roof slope, again bringing it over the ridge so it overlaps the first piece. On wider roofs the felt will not reach from eaves to ridge; in this situation, lay a third strip along the ridge so it overlaps the two lengths lower down the roof slopes. Cut the felt at the corners of the roof, and fold and tack the overlaps down neatly. Turn the lower edges of the felt over the edges of the roof boards, tack them and fit a fascia board. Fit a gable end cut from wide board or exterior-grade plywood (3), then finish off by glazing the window, hanging the door and applying an overall coat of preservative (4).

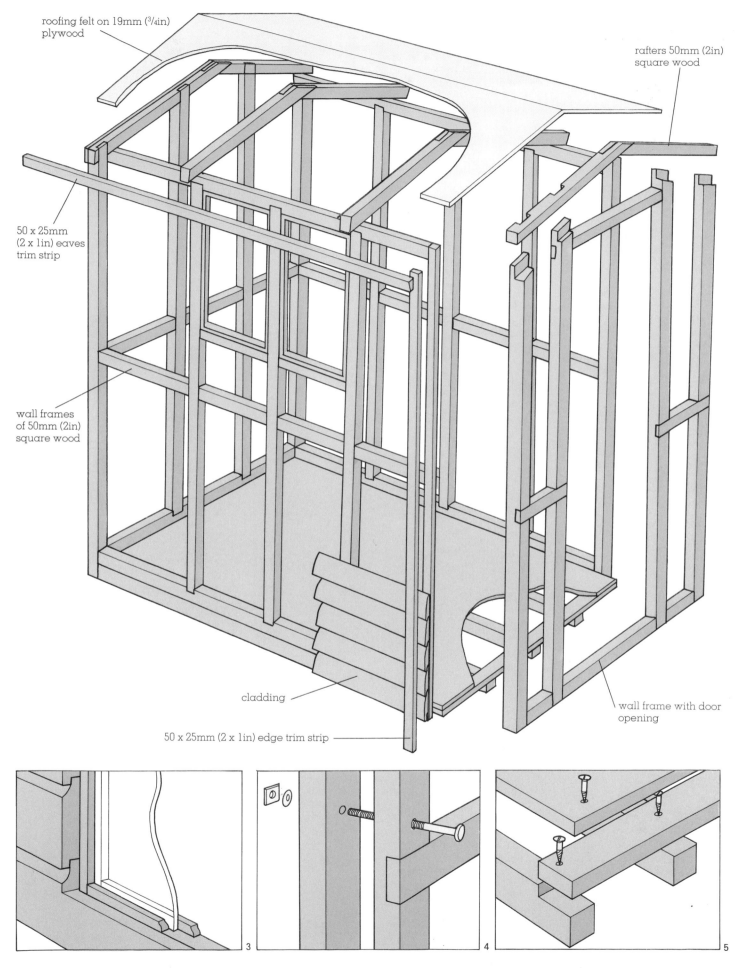

roofing felt on 19mm (³/₄in) plywood

rafters 50mm (2in) square wood

50 x 25mm (2 x 1in) eaves trim strip

wall frames of 50mm (2in) square wood

cladding

wall frame with door opening

50 x 25mm (2 x 1in) edge trim strip

3

4

5

Play Equipment

All children enjoy playing out of doors, especially if the garden contains some special play equipment round which they can develop their own games. Wood is an excellent material to use for equipping a play area, whether you are making just a simple sandpit or a more elaborate construction such as a climbing frame or tree house. It is strong, easy to fix, clean and above all safe in use, so long as you take care to smooth all surfaces and round off all edges so they are splinter-free. You must also take steps to ensure that whatever you make is securely anchored to the ground so it cannot move or topple over.

Building a Sandpit

As every family knows, children love the seaside – especially a sandy beach, where they can dig and build to their heart's content. The trouble is that for most families the seaside is too far away for more than the occasional trip. The answer is to provide a bit of beach in your back garden, in the form of a sandpit, where they can play whenever they want.

Building a permanent sandpit in the garden is a perfect do-it-yourself job, and a good opportunity to practise your woodworking skills on a relatively simple project. It can be raised or sunken (the latter is even easier to construct than the former), and can be turned into an ornamental pond or planter once the children outgrow it.

Siting a Sandpit

There are two points to take into consideration when you are deciding where to put your sandpit. The first is safety: you really need to be able to keep an eye on its occupants from the house, so having it in view from the kitchen window is the ideal answer. The second is tidiness; sandpits have a habit of spreading their contents over a fairly wide area, so surrounding the pit with a hard surface such as paving or giving it a wide seat all round will make it easier to sweep up straying sand at the end of the day. Try to avoid putting it under a tree, where resin and bird droppings could fall on its occupants in summer (autumn leaves are not such a problem – the season is not so popular for outdoor games anyway).

Designing a Sandpit

If you plan a raised pit, aim to make the sides about 380mm (15in) high so even tiny tots can climb in on their own. Similarly, a sunken pit needs about the same depth of sand. As far as other dimensions go, it really depends on the size of your garden, but a practical minimum is about 1.2m (4ft) square. Make it bigger if you can.

Choosing Materials

You can surround a sandpit in several ways, two of which are illustrated here. One is to set logs on end in the ground, butting them closely together to form a palisade round the pit area. The other is to use planed timber to build a purpose-made pit in the form of a timber box with

Left: A generous allocation of space for play will take pressure off the rest of the garden.

Above: *Designed with a young family in mind, this town garden provides a safe play area for all ages.*

extended sides that help to stop the sand straying and also act as a seat.

As far as sand is concerned, the best type is washed silver sand, which is available from builders' merchants. On no account use bricklaying or concreting sand, which will stain clothes and hands horribly. If you live near the seaside, you may be tempted to 'borrow' some sackfuls of your local beach sand; this is also not recommended since it will have a high salt content which can make little hands sticky and sore. You need enough sand to fill the pit to a depth of about 225mm (9in): if it's any deeper, a lot more will find its way out of the pit over the sides. So for a pit 1.2m square you'll need about a third of a cubic metre (yard) of sand. Scale the figure up accordingly for larger pits. The last items on your materials list are designed to stop the sandpit from turning into a bog in wet weather, and to prevent local pets from using it as a toilet (with potentially unpleasant consequences for your children's health). To allow rainwater to drain through the sand bed, fill the base of the pit with about 50mm (2in) of gravel, topped with a sheet of heavy-duty polyethylene that you have perforated with small holes every 100mm (4in) or so (a small electrician's screwdriver is ideal for this). The polyethylene layer also discourages would-be human moles from digging too deep. To cover the pit at night and to keep animals from using it as a toilet, make a matching wooden cover which can simply be lifted into place.

Play Equipment

Building a sunken pit

Pick your site and mark out the extent of the excavation with pegs and string lines. Excavate the pit to a depth of about 300mm (12in), cutting the sides neatly and keeping them as vertical as possible. Look out for buried services as you dig, and reposition the pit if you find any. To line the walls of the pit area, you can drive in sharpened log stakes, butting them closely together to keep the sand in place and to stop the surrounding soil from collapsing into the pit, Alternatively, drive wooden stakes into the ground round the edge of the pit at, say, 900mm (3ft) intervals, then cut a sheet of exterior-quality plywood into strips, and nail them to the stakes to form a box with its top edge just below ground level. Smooth off and tamp down the base of the hole, then lay 50mm (2in) gravel covered by your poly-ethylene sheet. Finally shovel in the sand to the required depth.

Building a matching pit and tree seat

1 Choose your site, and strip away any turf or other vegetation first. Then mark out the site with string lines and pegs.
2 Next, drive in a fence spike at each corner of the construction, using an offcut of wood in the socket to protect it as you hammer it in. For the sandpit, add four more spikes at the corners of the pit area itself.
3 Cut the halving joint in the top of each 100mm (4in) square post as shown in the diagram, and secure it in its socket with nails or screws. Then prepare the main 100 x 50mm (4 x 2in) perimeter rails by cutting their ends at 45° and forming the halving joint cut-outs in two of them at roughly 450mm (18in) centres. Fit the perimeter rails, then cut the intermediate joists to length, form halvings on each end and nail them into place.
4 To fit the seat round a tree, add short trimmer joists at right angles to the main joists, then fit short joist sections as necessary to fill in the gap between the perimeter rails and the trimmer joists.

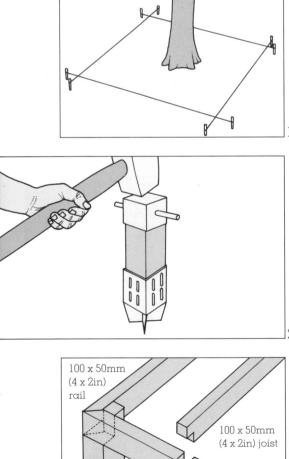

Right: *A matching tree seat, sandpit and swing – the perfect area in which the whole family can play or relax.*

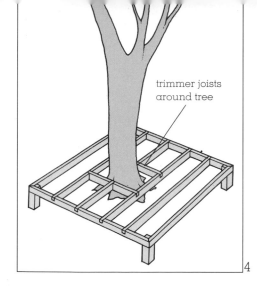

trimmer joists around tree

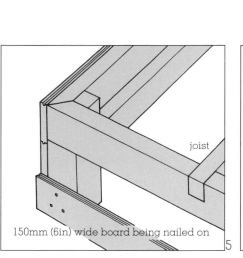

4

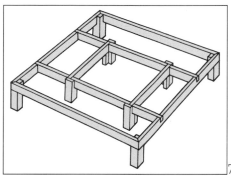

joist

150mm (6in) wide board being nailed on

5

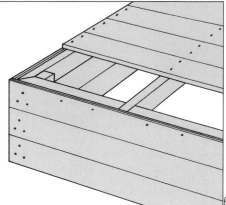

6

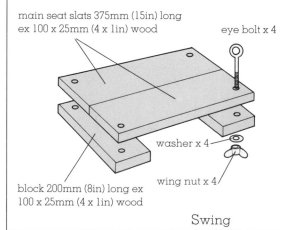

7

trimmer joist

50mm (2in) bearer

side rail

corner post

8

For the sandpit, add the rails round the pit area, and nail a 50mm (2in) square bearer to each post as shown in the diagrams (7, 8) to act as a fixing ground for the planks that will line the pit,

5 Now you can start nailing on the boards to form the sides of the structure and the pit, working from ground level upwards. Make sure that you recess the nail heads well using a punch.

6 Finish off by adding the boards forming the seat, nailing them to the perimeter rails and the joists. Finally lay gravel and a polythene sheet as for a sunken pit, fill with sand and fit a cover.

MAKING A COVER

Cut length of tongued-and-grooved timber cladding long enough to span the pit, assemble them and nail three 50 x 25mm (2 x 1in) battens across the back to hold them together and allow the completed cover to sit on the pit walls. Treat the wood with preservative to protect it from rot. Alternatively, use a piece of exterior-grade plywood, with battens pinned to it all round the underside to fit just within the pit walls. Again, treat it with preservative.

MAKING A SWING

The best place to site a swing is on the lawn; concrete and paved surfaces should be avoided at all costs, because of the risk of injuries resulting from a child falling from the swing itself.

This does mean, of course that the lawn will be badly worn immediately

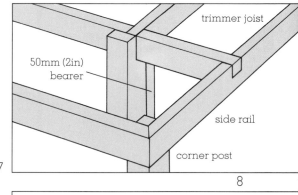

main seat slats 375mm (15in) long ex 100 x 25mm (4 x 1in) wood

eye bolt x 4

washer x 4

wing nut x 4

block 200mm (8in) long ex 100 x 25mm (4 x 1in) wood

Swing

below the swing as time goes by, and for this reason it is a good idea to surround the swing with an area of soft material such as bark chippings to cushion any falls. The swing itself needs to be well anchored to prevent it lifting as energetic acrobats swing back and forth. The swing shown here has its 100 x 50mm (4 x 2in) posts set in concrete to a depth of about 600mm (2ft), and so should be able to withstand even the most energetic swinging. When the concrete has set (see page 59 for more details), fit the crossbar, securing it with screws rather than nails, then drill holes and insert two large eyebolts to take the swing ropes. Use nylon rope, which will not rot, and fuse the knots together so they cannot pull undone by heating them up gently with a hot air gun until the plastic just begins to soften.

PLAY EQUIPMENT

PLAY BUILDINGS

Most children, given a free choice of outdoor play equipment, opt unerringly for a home of their own. Adventurous types with a head for heights are likely to request a tree house (assuming there is a suitably-sized tree in the garden in which to build it) where they and their friends can get away from grown-ups and indulge themselves in Tarzan or commando-type fantasies to their heart's content. Others may prefer a more down-to-earth approach and choose a conventional play house. This can be anything from a perfectly-built scaled-down replica of a summerhouse or chalet to a much more ramshackle home-made structure, perhaps built by the children themselves with a little adult supervision. Not only will such a shared project help to while away the holidays; it will give the children an immense sense of satisfaction to have been involved in buiiding their own

play equipment. It could also be a good way of using up all those leftovers from your own do-it-yourself projects which you could never bear to throw away.

Whatever type of building you decide to construct, remember that it must be a safe place for your children to play in. That means paying as much attention to its construction, finishing and security as you would to any other garden project.

CREATING A DRY BASE

For a start, anything built at ground level should have proper foundations – ideally a concrete slab, although with simple structures you might be able to get away with building 'direct to earth' as long as you can support the structure clear of the ground and so keep damp at bay. If you decide to lay concrete, you need a slab about 75mm (3in) thick, laid over 75-100mm (3-4in) of well-rammed rubble. Use a 1:2:3 cement:sand:aggregate mix (or 1:4 cement:combined

aggreates), and lay the concrete in formwork so the slab has neat square sides. This will then provide the perfect base for a timber floor off which the rest of the building can be constructed. For a more temporary structure, you can support the building's floor – tongue-and-grooved boards or exterior-grade plywood nailed to square joists – on rows of frostproof bricks, garden walling blocks or paving slabs. Tamp these down firmly into the soil, check that they are level with each other and then place a piece of something waterproof - roofing felt or plastic damp-course material – on top of each one. Before you lift the floor into position, it is a good idea to treat the ground underneath it to keep weeds under control. Lay black polythene sheeting over the supports, then set the floor in place on top of this.

ASSEMBLING THE BUILDING

Probably the best way of building up the structure from here is to follow the principles used by the manufacturers of prefabricated garden buildings, and to make up the individual wall panels with a simple frame covered in cladding. Use at least 50 x 25mm (2 x 1in) wood for the frame, and space uprights at about 450mm (18in) centres between the top and bottom plates to give the panel a reasonable degree of rigidity when the cladding is added. Exterior-grade plywood is probably the best cladding material to use, but you can press anything from old floorboards to fencing timber into service if you have it available. Fit cross-rails to form window and door openings, and then pin beading round the inside of the openings so the window can be glazed and the door has a stop bead to close against. Use the same material as for the walls to make up a matching door, with ledging and bracing on the inside, and hinge it to the door post. Either fit a simple hook and eye inside and out to keep the door shut, or fit a surface mounted latch and door handles if the budget will run to it.

Glaze windows with unbreakable rigid plastic sheet, held in place with beading all round. Use PVC tape to simulate glazing bars. With an extra pair of hands to help you steady the panels, lift the first one onto the edge of the floor. Then place the next panel at right angles to the first and fix the two together by nailing through the end frame uprights. Repeat the process to fit the third and fourth panels, then nail the bottom plate of each wall panel securely to the floor.

THE FRAMEWORK

purlin

rafters

purlin

plywood floor nailed to
75 x 25mm (3 x 1in) joists

wall frames of
50 x 25mm (2 x 1in) wood

Right: A "Wendy House" will provide hours of entertainment. This one is large enough to become a wet-weather play area and den for older children.

ADDING THE ROOF

The simplest type of roof you can fit is a flat roof consisting of a rectangle of exterior-grade plywood, cut to overhang the walls by about 50mm (2in) all round. Give it a slight slope so rainwater drains off it. To do this, carefully saw a length of 100 x 50mm (4 x 2in) wood in half to form two matching strips tapering from 50mm (2in) thick at one end to nothing at the other. Nail one on top of each side wall, with the thicker ends at the front of the building, and add a length of 50mm (2in) square wood along the top of the front wall. Place the roof in position and nail it down all round. Then cover it with roofing felt, secured with galvanized clout (roofing) nails. Turn the felt over the edge of the roof and tack it underneath the eaves. Make sure the nails do not protrude through the roof decking. If your building has a pitched roof, you can again use plywood but you really need to provide some support along the ridge line – few children can resist climbing on the roof of their 'castle' sooner or later. To avoid complex carpentry, the simplest solution is to form a home-made joist hanger from three offcuts of wood nailed in a U-shape to the inside of the apex on each side wall panel, and then to drop in a ridge board – length of 75 x 50mm (3 x 2in) or 100 x 50mm (4 x 2in) wood – so its top corners are level with the tops of the panels. Secure the board by driving a 100mm (4in) woodscrew through each side wall into the ends of the board, then position the roof panels and nail the top edge of each one to the ridge board, the other edges to the tops of the wall panels. Cover the roof with two strips of roofing felt, laid so each just extends over the ridge to give a double layer of waterproofing at the roof's weakest spot.

Right: *A good substitute for the ever popular treehouse, which requires a substantial and suitably-sited tree.*

Below: *This Scandinavian-style playhouse would make an attractive feature in any garden. Scaled up it would work equally well as a summerhouse.*

Planters and Window Boxes

Although most gardeners' natural inclination is to plant things directly in the ground, there is plenty of scope for an alternative approach — using man-made planters above ground level as a garden feature in their own right. Wood is a splendid material for this, since it gives you the chance to design and construct plant containers in all sorts of styles rustic or formal and in whatever shape or size you want. You can leave the wood its natural colour, stain it or paint it if you prefer; the latter choice is particularly popular for window boxes, where you want the container to match the house décor.

Above: *Wooden barrels make a wonderful show when planted with colourful annuals.*

Left: *This low wooden building has been much improved by the addition of white-painted boxes.*

You need little more than imagination and some very basic raw materials to create attractive and unusual planters for your garden. The basic requirements are to contain the planting medium soil or compost so rain does not wash it out, and to ensure that there is adequate drainage to prevent the planter from becoming waterlogged. Depending on the type of planter you are creating and any decorative finish you want to give it, you may also need to devise ways of keeping the wood out of contact with the soil by fitting some sort of liner inside the plant container.

Perhaps the simplest type of planter you can create uses 'raw' wood as a building material. For example, you could simply nail logs together into a trough shape, with short pieces filling in the ends, and stand the resulting container on two more logs to lift it clear of the ground, as shown in the picture above. Use fine gravel to fill the uneven joints between the logs, then firm in your planting medium ready for whatever you propose to grow.

An even simpler trick is to make use of ready made containers such as traditional wooden barrels cut in half – a favourite feature of many a cottage style garden, especially if they are painted white with a contrasting colour on the metal hoops as shown in the main picture. All you need to do to convert one into a planter is to drill some holes in the bottom of the barrel for drainage, then to line it with heavy duty black polyethylene sheeting held in place with staples to stop the wood being permanently saturated and therefore prone to rot. Pierce the sheeting where it

covers the drainage holes, and fill the bottom of the barrel with a layer of gravel and small stones to prevent the planting medium from clogging the drainage holes. Then position the barrel clear of the ground on bricks, for example and fill it up with soil or compost ready for planting.

You can create more substantial garden planters by using large section sawn timbers, such as old fashioned wooden railway sleepers (ties), built up into retaining walls round flowerbeds or as free standing planters. Wood of this size is massive enough to need no fixings; its own weight will keep it in place. Old railway sleepers, if you can get hold of them, are ideal for this type of garden construction because they are heavily impregnated with wood preservative and so will not rot. Alternatively, contact local demolition contractors, who often save large section timber when knocking down old houses. Once you have positioned the lengths to create the structure you want with the aid of a helper (they are very

heavy), all you have to do is to fill it up with soil. Since they are sawn timber, they will fit together closely enough, so need no lining.

You can of course use your woodworking skills to make planting troughs in any shape and design you want (see page 77 for an example). One place where such planters can look particularly attractive is on window sills, if yours are wide enough to support a window box. Obviously, each window box has to be tailor made to suit its sill, but the basic construction can be very simple – just a long narrow box. The project overleaf shows you how you can make one.

The base of a window box can be solid wood or exterior-grade plywood, with holes drilled through it for drainage, or you can form a slatted bottom by spacing the pieces about 6mm (^{1}/4in) apart. Treat it thoroughly with clear wood preservative if you want to paint it, or with a coloured preservative wood stain otherwise, paying special attention to any exposed endgrain which is particularly prone to rot. Line the box with polyethylene sheeting, stapled into place, and pierce holes in it across the bottom before filling it with soil or compost. Alternatively, omit the lining; instead, simply plant out a number of square flower pots and stand them side by side in the trough.

Remember that all window boxes must be secured to the sill so they cannot fall or be knocked off accidentally. The simplest fixing is to use an L-shaped metal repair bracket at each side, screwed to the box and to the sill.

Left: *Rustic-style planter best constructed in situ and lifted off the ground to delay rot.*

Below: *Old railway sleepers have been used to form large, easily maintained, raised bed planters.*

Planters and Window Boxes

Making a window box

You can make this simple yet stylish window box from natural timber or a suitable man-made board, 19mm (³/₄in) thick. The dimensions given in the cutting list are for a box 762mm (30in) long, 197mm (7³/₄in) high and 203mm (8in) from front to back, but you can vary the dimensions to suit any sill.

Cut the components to size, then cut 3mm (¹/₈in) deep housings across the inner face of the front and back pieces, 12mm (¹/₂in) from each end – a perfect job for a power router. The sides of the box will slot into these grooves when it is assembled. Cut another groove on these components along the bottom of the inner face, again 12mm (¹/₂in) from the edge. Finally, cut a similar groove along the bottom of the inner face of each end piece. These grooves will hold the bottom of the box.

Now you can start the assembly. Glue and pin the bottom into the groove in the back, then add the two ends and slot on the front, again gluing and pinning the joints to complete the basic box shape.

To finish the box off, cut the three sections that make up the top frame from 38 x 19mm (1¹/₂ x ³/₄in) wood, trim them to 45° and pin and glue them into place.

If the box is to contain soil rather than flower pots, drill drainage holes in the bottom and line it with polyethylene to keep the box free from rot.

Cutting list

A: The box
Back 762 x 197 x 19mm (30 x 7³/₄ x ³/₄in)
Front 762 x 177 x 19mm (30 x 7 x ³/₄in)
Ends 172 x 177 x 19mm (6³/₄ x 7 x ³/₄in)
Base 705 x 172 x 19mm (27³/₄ x 6³/₄ x ³/₄in)

B: The frame
Front 762 x 38 x 19mm (30 x 1¹/₂ x ³/₄in)
Ends 193 x 38 x 19mm (7⁵/₈ x 1¹/₂ x ³/₄in)

Assemble the box using waterproof wood working adhesive and 38mm (1¹/₂in) pins.

Left: *Finished planter painted white with small trees for formal effect.*

Left: *Painted bright red and planted for winter, the box makes a cheerful addition to an otherwise dull ledge.*

MAKING A PATIO PLANTER

This attractive patio planter is made from man-made board – exterior-grade plywood or medium-density fibreboard (MDF). It is basically a box with panelled sides, fitted with a removable top that neatly frames the planting area. The cutting list gives details of all the components; as with the window box, these can easily be varied to create a similar style planter of a different size.

Start by cutting all the components to size, and label them as per the cutting list. Then make up the four framed wall panels by gluing two rails and two stiles to each side. Note that opposite pairs of panels are slightly different sizes, denoted by A and B in the cutting list. Also note that the top and bottom rails fit flush with the edges of the side, while the stiles project by 12mm (¹⁄₂in). This forms strong overlapping corner joints when the four wall panels are pinned and glued together to form the basic box.

When you have assembled this, cut the base support battens to length and pin and glue them inside the box so they project below its bottom edge by about 10mm (³⁄₄in). Cut the base panel to size and glue and pin it to the top surface of the support battens. Complete the box by fitting the four internal corner battens, and drill a series of 6mm (¹⁄₄in) diameter drainage holes in the base.

Make up the top by gluing and cramping the four sections of 25mm (1in) thick board together. Then add the locating battens to frame the underside of its opening.

Sand it all down, then prime it and finish it with two coats of paint inside and out.

CUTTING LIST

Cut	12mm (¹⁄₂in) board
2 Sides A	425 x 426 (17 x 17in)
4 Stiles A	425 x 100 (17 x 4in)
2 Sides B	425 x 402 (17 x16in)
4 Stiles B	425 x 88 (17 x 3¹⁄₂in)
4 Top rails	250 x 75 (10 x 3in)
4 Bottom rails	250 x 100 (10 x 4in)
Cut	**25mm (1in) board**
1 Base panel	400 x 400 (16 x 16in)
2 Top pieces	550 x 100 (21 x 4in)
2 Top pieces	350 x 100 (13 x 4in)
Cut	**25 x 25mm (1 x 1in) timber**
4 Corner battens	360 (14in)
4 Base and top battens	400 (16in)
4 Base and top battens	350 (14in)

NOTE: Metric and Imperial dimensions are not interchangeable.

THERE ARE A LOT OF SMALLER-SCALE PROJECTS THAT THE KEEN WOODWORKER CAN TACKLE AROUND THE GARDEN, FROM MAKING FEEDING TABLES AND NESTING BOXES, TO BUILDING A COLD FRAME THAT WILL GIVE EARLY PLANTING A HEAD START. THESE PROJECTS ARE IDEAL FOR THE LONG WINTER EVENINGS, SINCE THEY CAN BE BUILT INDOORS AND THEN MOVED OUTSIDE WHEN SPRING ARRIVES. THEY ARE ALSO IDEAL FOR CHILDREN TO TACKLE, WITH A LITTLE ADULT SUPERVISION.

MAKING A BIRD FEEDING TABLE

This unusual feeding table is easy to make from a few offcuts of softwood and exterior-grade plywood. It is basically a hopper that dispenses food – through openings in the sides. It is filled by removing the roof, and the pyramid inside ensures that gravity keeps the food flowing.

Start by cutting out the feeding table floor a 305mm (12in) square of 16 or 19mm (⅝ or ¾in) thick plywood. Frame its edges by gluing and pinning on four neatly mitred 317mm (12½in) lengths of 30 x 6mm (1¼ x ¼in) beading, with their top edges flush with one face of the plywood.

Next, prepare the walls. Each is a 200 x 125mm (8 x 5in) piece of 12mm (½in)

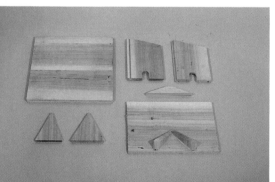

thick plywood, with a small door 35mm (1⅜in) high and 25mm (1in) wide cut into one edge with a coping saw. The top edges of each wall panel are cut away to an angle of 70° – a job for a protractor. Glue the four pieces together in sequence so that the face of one piece overlaps the edge of the next as you work round the square. Then glue the assembled walls to the table at a 45° angle to its edges.

Now you can turn your attention to the roof. Cut two pieces of 12mm (½in) plywood measuring 305 x 200mm (12 x 8in), and mark up and cut out the two gables – each a triangle with a base length of 175mm (6⅞in) and a height of 35mm (1⅜in), cut from 19mm (¾in) plywood. Plane off one long edge of each roof section to an angle of 70° and test that the planed edges meet neatly when a gable end is held against their undersides. Glue the gable ends into place about 25mm (1in) from the edges of the roof. Then cut some scrap wood blocks and glue them to the underside of the roof to locate it in place. They should be a reasonably tight fit inside the walls.

Finally, make the pyramid to fit loosely inside the house, either by gluing four triangles of plywood together or by shaping it from a soild block. It measures 110mm (4⅜in) square.

The stand is made from a 1.4m (4ft 7in) length of 50mm (2in) square planed timber, and is located in a socket on the underside of the table formed with scrap wood. The feet are two 510mm (20in) lengths of 50 x 19mm (2 x ¾in) wood, joined at right angles with a cross-halving joint. They are linked to the stand with four triangular braces cut from 75 x 50mm (3 x 2in) softwood, which are glued and screwed into place.

In windy locations, weight the feet down or dispense with them altogether and set the post in concrete or a fence post socket, instead.

Right: *Painted green and white, the bird feeding table will brighten up any winter garden.*

Left: *This rustic-style bird table with shingle roof has been treated with wood preservative.*

MAKING A NEST BOX AND FEEDING TABLE

This design combines an open feeding table with a nesting box – an essentially decorative touch, since only the least choosy birds will actually nest over a feeding table. Once again, begin with the table – a 305mm (12in) square of 16 or 19mm (⁵/₈ or ³/₄in) plywood, edged with mitred 317mm (12¹/₂in) lengths of 30 x 6mm (1¹/₄ x ¹/₄in) hardwood beading. Drill four 10mm (³/₈in) diameter holes in it at 200mm (8in) centres so you can dowel-joint the roof posts to it.

The four posts are 185mm (7¹/₄in) lengths of 30mm (1¹/₄in) square softwood. Drill a 10mm (³/₈in) diameter hole in one end of each post and glue in a length of 10mm (³/₈in) dowel so it projects by the thickness of the feeding table. At the other end, make a cut-out 15mm (⁵/₈in) square, and then cut the projecting stub off at an angle of 45° as shown in the components photograph. Glue the posts in their holes so that opposite pairs of cut-outs face inwards towards each other.

Next, cut out the nest box floor – a 230 x 200mm (9 x 7⁷/₈in) piece of 12mm (¹/₂in) plywood, and glue it into the notches in the tops of the posts.

Now you can start work on the roof. First mark up and cut out two gables. Each is a triangle with a base length of 232mm (9¹/₈in) and a height of 140mm (5¹/₂in), and has a 40mm (1⁵/₈in) diameter opening drilled in it about 25mm (1in) below the top of the triangle. One also has a dowel perch glued into a further

hole just below the opening. Cut a third triangle to the same shape but measuring 38mm (1¹/₂in) less across the bottom, to act as a divider between the nesting compartments, and glue it across the middle of the nest box floor.

The roof itself consists of tongued-and-grooved softwood boards, glued together and then cut into two panels measuring 320mm (12¹/₂in) wide and 260mm (10¹/₄in) high. After assembling them, bevel one long edge of each panel to 45°. Then cut a 267mm (10¹/₂in) length of 30mm (1¹/₄in) triangular moulding to act as the ridge board, and glue the roof panels, gables and ridge board together. Glue the wider face of a 280mm (11in) length of 19mm (³/₄in) triangle moulding to the underside of the roof slope at the point where the base of the gable meets the roof, and add similar pieces of 15mm (⁵/₈in) moulding to the edges of the nesting box floor between the roof posts as shown in the photographs. Finally, fit the roof. The post is the same as for the other feeding table described on this page.

Above: *Painted blue and white, the feeding table makes an attractive and practical addition to any garden.*

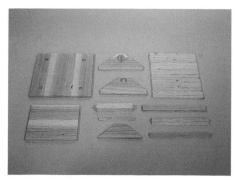

Making an Aviary

If you keep caged birds such as budgerigars, you can add a touch of colour to your garden by making them a summer aviary such as the one featured here. It is designed as a mobile unit, so you can roll it into the sun or the shade as required, and also 'drive' it into the garage and close the door before you transfer the birds to their indoor cages.

The structure could not be simpler. It consists of four corner posts of 50mm (2in) square timber, linked at top, centre and bottom by four 50mm (2in) square rails. All the joints are simple halving joints, glued and screwed together. With the framework assembled, the next step is to glue and nail lengths of 50 x 25mm (2 x 1in) wood to the outer faces of the top, centre and bottom rails on three sides of the structure; leave the back unadorned, ready to be covered with a full-length panel of 12mm (½in) thick exterior-grade plywood, which is glued and nailed to the posts and rails all round. Another panel forms the floor, again simply glued and nailed into place to the underside of the four bottom rails.

The roof consists of two panels of plywood cut to overlap the eaves and gable ends by about 50mm (2in) all round. Use a power saw to cut some 50mm (2in) square wood lengthwise into right-angled triangles. Then glue and nail a length to the upper face of each top side rail to act as a roof support, and use another length as a ridge board to link the two roof panels at right angles to each other. Set the assembled roof panels in place on the aviary and nail through them into the triangular roof supports. Then cut two gable pieces to fit and nail them to the ends of the ridge board and the roof supports at the front and back of the structure.

The next job is to line the inside of the door opening with 38 x 25mm (1½ x 1in) wood all round, fitted flush with the front faces of the corner posts and horizontal rails, and then to make up the door to fit the opening. Use 38mm (1½in) square wood for this, using either halving or mitre joints at the corners, and hinge it to the lining at one side. Add a hasp and staple at the other side.

Now you can cut the mesh to size, but do not fit it until you have painted the structure inside and out. Once the paint has dried, staple the mesh into place. Note that the upper section is in one piece for security. Measure up the length of the three sides of the aviary internally, then cut the mesh to the length and height required and make the two 90° folds in it on your workbench. Then manoeuvre the section inside the aviary, and start fixing one end to one of the rear corner posts. Next, staple it to the horizontal side rails, working towards the adjacent corner post. Hold the first fold against the post and staple it there, then take the mesh across the front of the aviary to the other front corner post and finally back to the other rear corner post. Staple the top and bottom edges carefully to the top and centre rails.

Complete the mesh work by cutting panels to fit the two lower side wall sections and the door, and staple them in place too. Last of all, fit the castors, screwing them through the floor panel into the bottom ends of the corner posts.

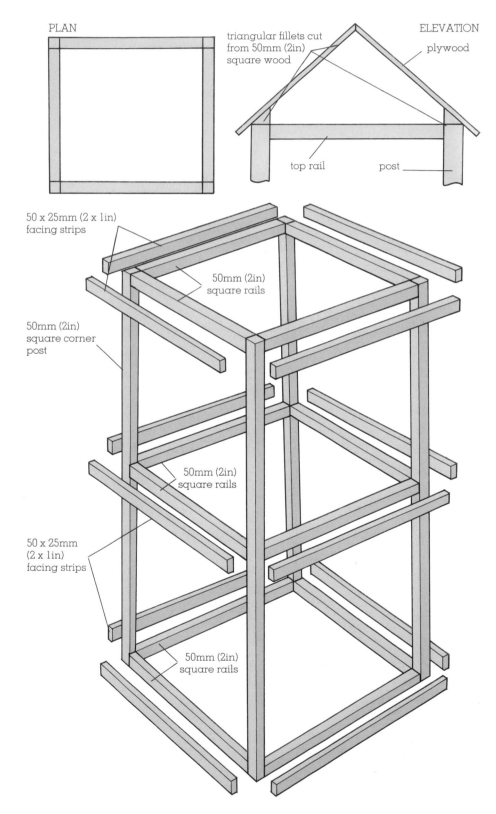

PLAN

triangular fillets cut from 50mm (2in) square wood

ELEVATION

plywood

top rail

post

50 x 25mm (2 x 1in) facing strips

50mm (2in) square rails

50mm (2in) square corner post

50mm (2in) square rails

50 x 25mm (2 x 1in) facing strips

50mm (2in) square rails

Right: This summer aviary for your budgies can be moved around easily. Be careful not to leave it in full sun.

Small Weekend Projects

Making a cold frame

If you want to give seeds a head start or protect delicate cuttings, a cold frame is the ideal structure for preventing a touch of frost from nipping them in the bud. This one is made from tongued-and-grooved softwood cladding, fixed to sturdy corner posts, and has two opening top frames. Apart from the usual woodworking tools, you will find a router or a set of shaping cutters for your electric drill invaluable for making the opening frames. Start by cutting the 19mm (³/4in) thick cladding to length – 1169mm (46in) long for the front and back, and 578mm (22³/4in) long for the ends. Glue and cramp the boards together to make up panels which you can then cut down to exactly the required height – 406mm (16in) for the back and 353mm (13⁷/8in) for the front. Mark the ends to be 353mm (13⁷/8in) high at the front and 406mm (16in) high at the back, link the marks with a cutting line and saw along it. Use a plane to bevel the top edge of the front and back panels off to an angle of about 20°.

Make up the centre strut next from one 578mm (22⁷/8in) length and one 588mm (23¹/8in) length of 75 x 19mm (3 x ³/4in) wood, plus one 537mm (21¹/8in) length of 25 x 15mm (1 x ⁵/8in) wood. Glue and screw the two wider pieces together to form a beam with a cross-section in the shape of a T, aligning them at one end so that the other end of the on-edge piece of wood projects by 10mm (³/8in). This stub on the upper end of the strut locates in a vertical blind mortise cut in the middle of the back panel, with the top of the cut-out 44mm (1³/4in) below the top edge of the back panel. Then glue and screw the 25 x 15mm length of wood on edge on top of the assembled T-section so it projects 44mm (1³/4in) beyond the lower end of the T-section strut.

Now you can cut the corner posts to length from 45mm (1³/4in) square wood. You need two 406mm (16in) long and two 353mm (13⁷/8in) long. Glue and screw them to the corresponding side edges of both the end panels, and then screw the back and front panels to the posts so the ends of these two panels overlap the exposed endgrain of the two end panels. Slot one end of the centre strut into its mortise in the back panel, then screw through the front panel into its other end to secure it in position. Finally, add the top back rail to which the opening frames will be hinged; this is a 1199mm (47in) length of 85 x 25mm (3³/8 x 1in) wood which is screwed to the tops of the corner posts and also to the centre strut.

The components of the glazed frames are cut from 25mm (1in) thick wood. The

two sides are 572mm (22¹/2in) long and 50mm (2in) wide, and each has a 9mm (³/8in) wide groove cut 12mm (¹/2in) deep along its inner edge to hold the glass. The back rail, which is hinged to the top back rail of the cold frame, is a 538mm (21¹/4in) length of 75mm (3in) wide wood, also grooved and with 25mm (1in) long tenons cut on each end so the width between the tenon shoulders is 488mm (19¹/4in). The front rail is 588mm (23¹/8in) long and 80mm (3¹/8in) wide, and has a 50 x 12mm (2 x ¹/2in) rebate machined along its length.

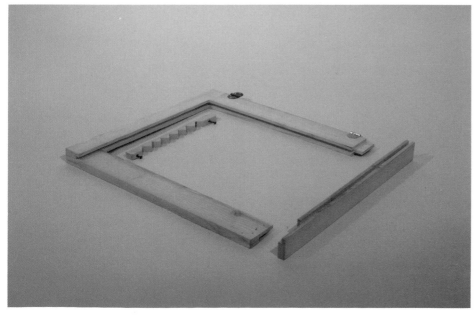

Above: *Attractively painted, the cold frame becomes a practical and attractive addition to any garden.*

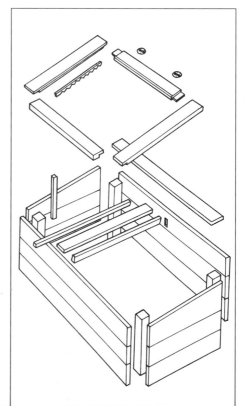

The top corner joint of each frame is an open mortise joint, while the bottom corner joints are halving joints; this allows the glass to oversail the front rail, which itself overlaps the front wall of the cold frame. This is to allow water to run off and drip away from the front.

Assemble the frames, slide in the glass – a pane measuring 506 x 490mm (19⁷/₈ x 19¹/₄in) – and secure the bottom edge of the pane to the bottom rail of the frame with glazing sprigs to keep it in place. Finally hinge the frames to the top back rail of the cold frame.

Hand Tools

IN AN AGE WHERE THE POWER TOOL IS KING, IT IS EASY TO FORGET THE ARRAY OF HAND TOOLS AVAILABLE TO THE DO-IT-YOURSELFER. HERE IS A GUIDE TO SOME OF THE HAND TOOLS YOU MIGHT NEED FOR YOUR OUTDOOR ACTIVITIES.

Hand tools

Perhaps the simplest of all woodworking jobs is fixing things together. In each case you have to make a fixing of some sort – either driving a nail or a screw. Nails are easier to use than screws; all you need to drive them is a hammer (see below). However, it is not always easy to drive nails exactly where you want them, and it is difficult to get them out again once they are in. Screws are better: they provide a more secure grip, and can be undone easily if you want to move or change whatever it is that you have fixed. However, you need separate tools to make the hole and to drive the screw.

Drills

Requirement number one is a drill. For this job there is little point in buying a hand drill; invest in an electric drill, ideally one with a 13mm (¹/₂in) chuck,

variable speed control and hammer action, so you can tackle a wide range of drilling jobs in all sorts of materials with just one tool. See page 86 for more details.

For actually making the holes, you need some drill bits. Buy high speed steel twist drills for making holes in wood, plus two or three masonry drills for making holes in walls. Twist drills are sized in millimetres or in fractions of an inch, and are sold in sets as well as singly. Masonry drills are sized by numbers that match screw gauges, or in millimetres.

Screwdrivers

For driving the screws, you need a screwdriver. To be precise, you need several screwdrivers, because screws come in several sizes and have heads of different types. For the driver to work efficiently, its blade must match the slot or recess in the screw head. If it slips out, it will damage whatever you are fixing.

You can probably get by with just two flat-bladed screwdrivers of different sizes for driving slotted screws, plus one cross-point driver for cross-head screws (Pozidriv and Supadriv are the commonest types; a No 2 size screwdriver will drive the most widely-used screw sizes). Most screwdrivers nowadays have plastic handles; choose ones that feel comfortable in your hand.

Measuring and marking tools

There are several other tools you will find invaluable. The first is a retractable steel measuring tape, to help you get things the right size or the right distance apart and at the right height. Choose one with a tape at least 3.5m (12ft) long, marked with both metric and imperial measurements; it is a good idea to have one with a lock so you can take long measurements without the tape coiling up unexpectedly.

The second tool is a spirit level, invaluable for ensuring that you fix things like posts truly vertical and get rails and other components at a true horizontal. Choose one about 900mm (3ft) long with a metal body and both horizontal and vertical indicators; then you can use it for getting things plumb too. Add a pencil, so you can mark the positions of screw holes, draw guide lines and so on.

The third tool you will need is a try square, used for marking cutting lines at right angles to the edge of the wood you are cutting to length.

Hammers

Despite the superiority of screws for making secure fixings, a hammer is a tool you cannot do without. Choose a claw hammer, which can pull nails out as well as drive them. One with a metal shaft and a moulded rubber handgrip will stand up to more abuse than one with a traditional wooden shaft.

A tenon saw

Even if you plan to do no more carpentry than cutting a few battens to length, you must have a saw. A tenon saw will cope with most small sawing jobs on thin boards and on timber up to about 50mm (2in) thick. Choose one with a 300 or 350mm (12 to 14in) blade and a plastic handle which will not split or crack like a wooden one.

For heavier-duty sawing, either buy a power saw (see page 86) or a hand saw. The cross-cut saw has a blade 600–650mm (23–26in) long with between six and eight points (teeth) per inch, and as its name implies is ideal for heavy-duty cutting across the grain. For ripping

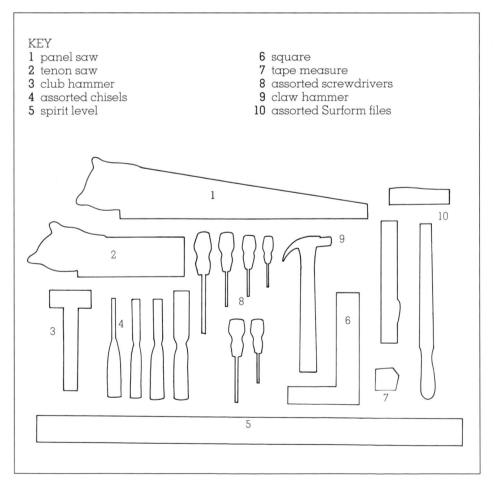

KEY
1 panel saw
2 tenon saw
3 club hammer
4 assorted chisels
5 spirit level
6 square
7 tape measure
8 assorted screwdrivers
9 claw hammer
10 assorted Surform files

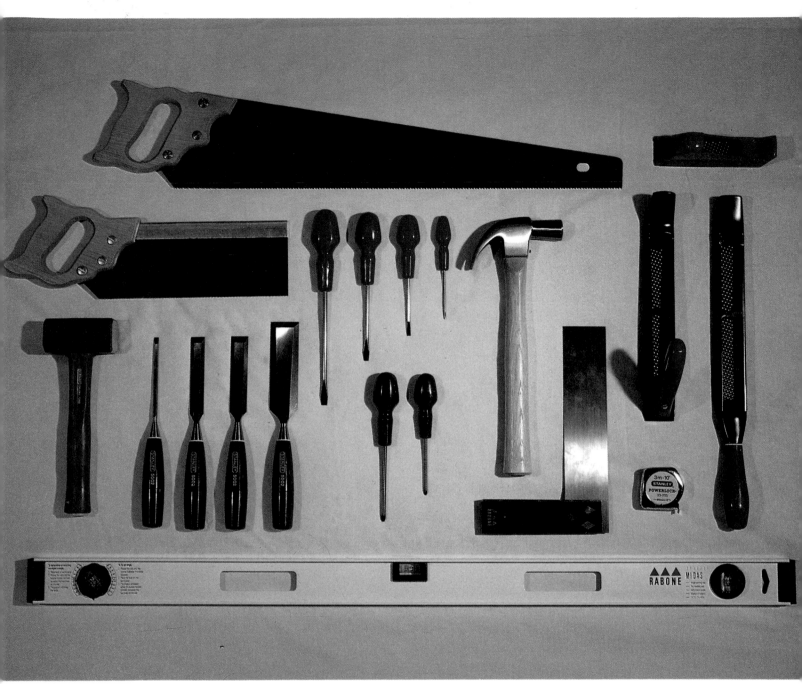

wood along the grain direction, use a rip saw instead; this has fewer teeth per inch, and the teeth are chisel-shaped rather than knife-shaped as on a cross-cut saw.

A SURFORM

There are likely to be a variety of wood-shaping jobs you will have to tackle. A Surform, which is a general purpose plane/rasp, is ideal for this. Surforms come in a range of styles, including flat rasps, planer-files, round files and block planes. All have replaceable blades.

TOOLS FOR CUTTING JOINTS

When it comes to cutting joints, recesses for hinges and so on, a set of wood chisels is essential. Bevel-edge chisels are more versatile than firmer chisels because you can undercut with them; you need at least four, in 6, 12, 18 and 25mm ($^1/_4$, $^1/_2$, $^3/_4$ and 1in) widths. Choose plastic handles rather than wooden ones, so you can drive them with your claw hammer instead of a mallet. You will need an oilstone to keep them sharp. See pages 90–91 for more details of how to make three essential wood-working joints.

ADJUSTABLE SPANNERS (WRENCHES)

You are likely to be using nuts and bolts to assemble some of the larger outdoor woodwork structures featured in this book. Obviously, in an ideal world you would have a different spanner for every nut, but a couple of adjustable spanners will do just as well; you need two because often you will have to grip a nut as well as a bolt. Choose one small and one medium spanner, to enable you to cope with a wide range of different nut and bolt sizes.

A PAIR OF PLIERS

Pliers are a real jack-of-all-trades tool – they will grip all sorts of things you may be trying to undo or tighten up, and will also bend things like stiff wire. Choose a pair of combination pliers with fine and coarse serrated jaws and a wire cutter near the pivot point; plastic hand grips make them more comfortable to use.

wood and 12mm (¹/₂in) or so in masonry. Most two-speed drills now have hammer action as well.

You get even more versatility with variable-speed drills, since you can choose precisely the right speed for the job you are doing and also vary it if necessary while you are working. Variable-speed drills have either one or two speed ranges, the latter being selected by a mechanical gearbox. Others also have reverse gear with variable speed control which is useful for repetitive jobs like undoing screws. Hammer action is a feature of most variable-speed drills. Most have 13mm (¹/₂in) chucks, although some heavy duty models with 16mm (⁵/₈in) chucks are available in 'professional' ranges.

Cordless drills running on internal rechargeable batteries are now very popular, especially as a second drill, because of the convenience of not having to use an extension lead. They are especially useful for work on cars, boats and caravans as well as for jobs in the garden away from a convenient power source. They run much more slowly than a mains-operated drill, but they are still capable of drilling holes up to around 19mm (³/₄in) in wood, 10 or 12mm (¹/₂in) in masonry. Some have two speeds or even variable speed control, and one or two models even feature hammer action. All cordless drills come complete with a charger unit, so the drill can be kept fully charged and ready for immediate use. Most also have reverse gear, making them ideal for removing screws too.

SANDERS

Power assistance is particularly useful for jobs like sanding, especially if you have large areas to tackle. You can choose between two types of power sander: the orbital sander and the belt sander.

An orbital sander has a flat rectangular baseplate covered with a soft cushion over which a sheet of abrasive paper is clipped or stuck. The sander's motor drives the baseplate via an eccentric pin mechanism; this makes it rotate in a sort of high-speed scrubbing action. Most orbital sanders are designed to accept either one-third or one-half of a standard-sized sheet of abrasive paper, which measures 280 x 230mm (11 x 9in). You can also get smaller models called palm-grip sanders; these accept a quarter-sheet of abrasive and are ideal for small areas where a larger tool cannot reach.

Most orbital sanders have motors rated at up to 250 watts and have a high orbit speed and small orbit diameter. This makes them ideal for finishing work, but they are not very good at removing large amounts of material. To

POWER TOOLS

Compare the average do-it-yourselfer's tool kit today with his grandfather's, and you would notice one huge difference: the power tools. Whereas grandfather did everything by hand, we now have the benefit of a wide range of power tools that take the hard work out of many of DIY jobs and in many cases mean we can achieve a more professional finish too. Here, briefly, is what each category of power tool has to offer.

DRILLS

The electric drill is without a doubt the most useful and versatile power tool. It will not only drill holes; it will also drive a wide range of attachments as well.

The simplest and least expensive type is the single-speed drill, which has a motor rated at about 400 watts and a chuck capacity of 10mm (³/₈in), giving it a drilling capacity of about 19mm (³/₄in) in wood. This makes it a good choice for light-duty drilling work. You can also get larger, more powerful models able to put up with heavy sustained use without burning out. Most have a larger 13mm (¹/₂in) chuck.

With two-speed drills you can choose a high speed for drilling wood and a lower one for metal and masonry, which makes this type generally more versatile than single-speed types. Two speed drills have either 10mm (³/₈in) or 13mm (¹/₂in) chucks, with the larger drills having motors rated at up to 600 watts. Drilling capacities for drills with 13mm (¹/₂in) chucks are around 25mm (1in) in do this you need either a more powerful motor, or else one with a lower orbit speed and larger orbit diameter. Some orbital sanders have variable speed control, and also have dust bags or a dust extraction facility.

Belt sanders have a continuous belt of abrasive that is guided round two rollers, and they can be used freehand or as a bench-mounted tool. They are altogether a heavier-duty machine than the orbital sander, and are capable of removing larger amounts of material much more quickly. However, a dust bag or dust extraction facility is essential to contain the resulting dust if you are working indoors, and belt sanders usually offer one or both options. Most models accept belts 65 or 75mm (2½ or 3in) wide, although larger professional models take belts 100mm (4in) wide. A few machines offer variable speed control.

JIG SAWS

The power jig saw is one of the most versatile of all power tools, since it can carry out all sorts of general-purpose cutting jobs. It can also double up as a coping saw or padsaw when you want to make cut-outs away from the edge of the wood, or to cut curves. You can fit a fence or use a guide batten to keep the saw on line when making long, straight cuts, and you can tilt the baseplate to make angled ones.

Most single-speed saws typically have motors rated at around 350 watts, giving cutting capacities of about 50mm (2in) in softwood. With variable-speed saws you have the option of using a slower speed setting which is essential if you are cutting curves or awkward shapes. They generally have more powerful motors than single-speed models – up to 550 watts or so – and their cutting capacity is generally greater too. You can expect to manage up to 70mm (2³/4in).

A variation on the jig saw has the blade projecting from the front end of the saw, enabling it to be used in the same manner as a handsaw and giving greater cutting capacity than a jig saw. It is variously known as the sabre saw or reciprocating saw, and can be fitted with different types of blades for fast or fine cutting. One step on from the sabre saw is a new type of saw with two reciprocating blades, rather like a hedge-trimmer, and which is virtually vibration-free.

CIRCULAR SAWS

Circular saws are mainly favoured by serious woodworkers who prefer to prepare their own timber instead of using off-the-peg sizes from the local timber merchant. They can be used free-

hand or can be mounted in a saw table for use as a bench saw. They have a tiltable soleplate, so you can make bevelled cuts, and can be fitted with an adjustable rip fence so accurate cuts can be made parallel to and a fixed distance away from the edge of the workpiece. Some models feature a dust extraction facility, like the jig saws mentioned earlier.

The smallest type of circular saw takes a 125mm (5in) diameter blade which gives a maximum cutting depth of around 30mm (1¼in), reducing to around 22mm (⁷/8in) for cuts made at an angle of 45°. Models taking 150mm (6in) blades have cutting depths of up to about 45mm (1³/4).

For heavier-duty work, you will need to turn to larger models rated at up to around 1000 watts. These accept blades about 180mm (7in) in diameter and are capable of cutting to depths of about 60mm (2³/8in). Most powerful of all are models taking 235mm (9¼in) diameter blades, giving a cutting depth in wood of up to 85mm (3³/8); their motors may be rated at up to 1500 watts, to provide the cutting power and speed required without risking burning out the motor.

Chop-saws are circular saws mounted on a baseplate and fitted with guides for cutting mitres and bevels accurately – useful for repetitive work. The workpiece is simply placed in the guides and the blade is lowered to make the cut.

ROUTERS

Routers are a favourite amongst specialist woodworkers, because the wide range of cutters available means you can cut a huge range of slots, grooves, chamfers, rebates and decorative profiles. The cutter rotates at extremely high speed – around 24,000rpm – and produces a clean fast cut so long as the cutters are sharp.

The majority of do-it-yourself routers are the plunge-action type, which means that the cutter is plunged down through the soleplate into the workpiece to start the cut – rather like using a drill stand.

POWER PLANERS

Power planers look rather like an ordinary bench plane, but there the similarity ends. The cutting action is provided by a rotating drum with two cutting blades which is mounted in the centre of the sole plate. The cutting depth is adjustable, and may range from about 0.5mm per pass on smaller models up to around 3mm (¹/8in) on more powerful machines. Most power planers have a cutting width of around 82mm (3¼in) – wider than a bench plane – and can cut chamfers and rebates as well.

PORTABLE WORKBENCH

If you are working out of doors and away from your workbench, you will find a portable foldaway workbench such as the world-famous Workmate invaluable. It is basically a huge vice on legs, with the flat timber jaws of the vice providing a work surface when closed. The jaws have holes designed to accept push-in plastic bench stops for planing and sawing jobs. A step platform lets you use your own weight to improve the bench's stability, and some models have fold-down legs which allow the work-surface height to be raised from sawhorse height to a more comfortable working level for other tasks. The long vice jaws are opened and closed by two independent screw mechanisms, so you can taper the gap to hold irregularly-shaped objects.

POST-HOLE BORERS

If you have a lot of posts set in the ground, a tool called a post-hole borer is well worth hiring from your local plant hire firm. It is basically a giant auger bit which literally drills out the hole as you turn the T-bar handle, and the resulting hole is both straight-sided and narrower than you can excavate with a spade. You can also get powered versions.

FIXING POSTS

Many of the projects featured in this book involve fixing posts securely in the ground, whether to support a run of fencing or to anchor a building or other structure. It is essential not to skimp on this job; if you do, the next spell of windy weather will simply flatten what you have built, often causing considerable damage to your garden and its contents in the process. Remember too that garden structures are unlikely to be covered by household insurance policies, so you will have to bear the expense of repair and reconstruction work yourself if the worst happens. Do the job properly in the first place and the problem will not arise.

There are two common ways of securing posts; to sink them in the ground and surround them with concrete, or to use metal fence spikes. In some countries, notably the US, galvanized post anchors are also widely used.

DIGGING HOLES

If you plan to sink your posts in the ground, the first thing you have to do is to make a hole for it. The golden rule is to sink approximately one-quarter of the overall post length in the ground; for example, a post that will project above ground by 1.8m (6ft) needs an additional 600mm (2ft) of post underground, so you must buy 2.4m (8ft) posts.

The hole needs to be a little deeper than a quarter of the post length so you can place some drainage material beneath it; add another 100mm (4in) to the overall hole depth to allow for it. This helps to prevent the foot of the post from being constantly waterlogged and therefore prone to rot, even if it has been treated with preservative first. As far as width is concerned, the ideal for a 100mm (4in) square post is a hole about 300mm (12in) across.

In firm, undisturbed ground it is relatively easy to dig a neat, square-sided hole with a garden spade, but in crumbly or recently-dug soil you may find that the sides tend to crumble as you dig. If this is the case, hiring a tool called a post-hole borer (see page 87) is well worth considering. Its rotating auger will drill out a cylindrical hole to whatever depth you require, and if the hand-operated types cannot cope with heavily-compacted or stony soil you can get petrol-engined borers that provide extra digging power. However, neither can cope with a really rocky subsoil; here you will probably have to turn to a pickaxe or even a pneumatic breaker to make any progress. It's worthwhile digging a few test holes with a spade to see what will be necessary.

GETTING THE POST VERTICAL

Once you have dug your hole to the depth you require, shovel in some gravel and bed half a brick or a piece of paving stone in the centre of it on which to stand the post. To set the post to the correct height, nail on a piece of scrap wood so this rests on the ground at each side of the hole when the post is stood in position. Adjust the level of the bedding brick in the gravel as necessary.

Next, cut two braces for each post from scrap wood, and fix them to adjacent sides of the post with a single nail through each brace, about two thirds of the way up the post. Adjust the brace positions until the post is standing vertically, then drive wooden pegs into the ground next to the foot of each brace and nail the brace to the peg (1). Double check that the post is still vertical. If you are setting posts to accept panel fencing, check the post spacing carefully at this stage too to ensure that the panels will fit once the posts are set in position (2). This checking may also apply for other garden structures where the correct post spacing is critical. It is not so important if you are putting up fencing with horizontal rails, since you can cut these to length to suit the actual post separation.

BEDDING THE POST IN PLACE

The next step is to concrete the post in place. The best method is to fill the hole completely with concrete, finishing the surface just below ground level so it slopes away from the post. This allows you to conceal the concrete with a thin layer of soil. However, you can reduce the amount of concrete this method requires by half-filling the hole with carefully-placed pieces of brick or stone, wedged against the faces of the post and well rammed down with a tamper or an offcut of fence post (3). Then top this off with concrete as before (4).

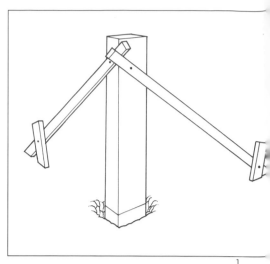

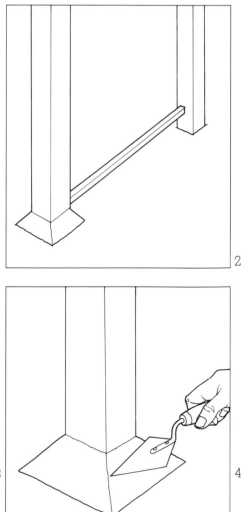

Use a 1:2½:3½ cement:sand:aggregate concrete mix, made with coarse 20mm (¾in) aggregate. If you are using combined aggregates, use a 1:5 mix. Add just enough water to moisten the mix, then shovel it into the hole and tamp it well down layer by layer. Give the surface a smooth finish with a trowel (4), then cover it with some soil to help retain moisture while the concrete sets. Leave this to harden for seven days before removing the braces and completing whatever structure the posts will support.

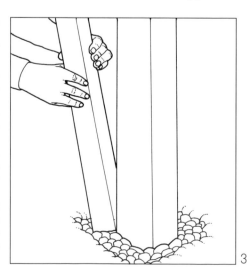

Using fence spikes

Fence spikes are a comparatively recent addition to fencing technology. They consist of a square metal socket welded to the top of a long spike, and are designed to be driven into the ground with a sledge hammer. To protect the socket from being damaged by the hammer blows, you either fit an accessory called a dolly – simply a steel block, sold along with the spikes – into the socket, or use a short offcut of fence post instead (1). You need a spike 600mm (24in) long for posts up to 1.2m (4ft) high, and a 760mm (30in) spike for 1.5 and 1.8m (5 and 6ft) posts. Sockets come in three sizes to accept 50, 75 and 100mm (2, 3 and 4in) square posts.

Once you have driven the spike into the ground, you simply set the post in the socket and secure it there by driving in screws or nails, or by tightening the mouth of the socket around the post with a spanner, according to the type of spike you are using (2).

Fence spikes offer a quick and relatively easy way of fixing posts. The main drawback is that it can be difficult getting the spike truly vertical; you need to keep checking that it is with a spirit level and a post offcut as you drive it into the ground, and to make adjustments if it is drifting off line. Spikes work best in dense, undisturbed soil that is comparatively free from buried stones and rocks, and should not be used for anchoring tall posts in exposed locations – anything over about 1.2m (4ft) high is best set in concrete.

Using post anchors

The post anchor is similar in principle to the fence spike. It is a galvanized steel socket into which the foot of the post fits, and is designed to be bolted to the top of a cylindrical concrete footing.

Dig the hole to the depth required by local building codes, than shovel some loose gravel into the bottom and set a concrete tube form in the hole after cutting it to the required length (3). Check that its top is level and about 50mm (2in) above ground level, then pack soil in round it to hold it upright.

Fill the tube form with concrete, tamping it down well and levelling it with the top of the form (4). Then set a J-bolt in the concrete at the centre of the footing so about 25mm (1in) of the threaded end is exposed (5), check that it is vertical with a spirit level and leave the concrete to set. When it has, cut away the exposed part of the tube form with a sharp utility knife.

Next, place the post anchor on the footing, slip the anchor plate over the J-bolt and tighten the nut down with a ratchet wrench (6). Then stand the post in the anchor and drive nails in through the pre-drilled fixing holes all round to lock it in position.

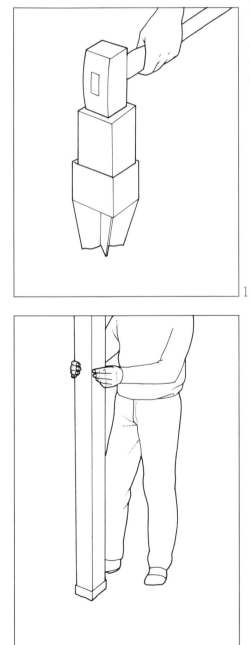

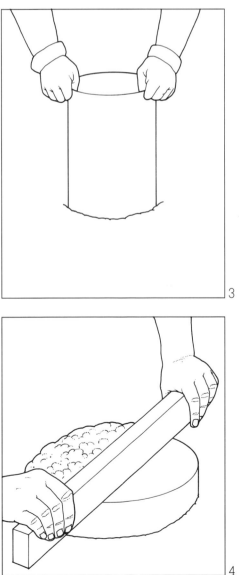

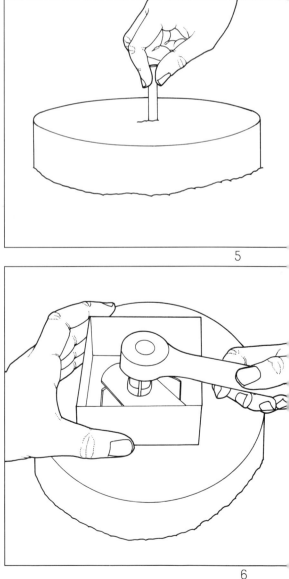

WOODWORKING JOINTS AND FIXINGS

Many of the garden structures featured in this book can be assembled using nothing more complicated than nails and butt joints. However, some will benefit from the additional strength and neatness of proper woodworking joints, in particular the halving joint and the mortise-and-tenon joint.

BUTT JOINTS

A butt joint, as its name implies, is formed by butting one component of the joint against the other, and then fixing the two together mechanically – usually with nails or screws. At corners and in T-joints, the end of the first component butts against the face of the second, through which the fixing nails or screws are driven (1).

As a general rule, butt joints should always be made by nailing through the thinner component into the thicker one, using a nail or screw about three times longer than the thickness of the thinner component. However, since the fixings pass into end-grain, the butt joint is not particularly strong and is prone to pulling apart under load if nails alone are used. For this reason, joints of this type are usually strengthened in some way. Gluing, using a waterproof adhesive, is one option. Skew-nailing (toe-nailing) involves driving the fixing nails at various opposing angles (2). In clench-nailing, over-long nails are driven right through the two components and their protruding points are then hammered flat to lock the components together. Butt joints can also be reinforced by fixing blocks inside the joint angle or adding reinforcing plates to the edges of the two components.

HALVING JOINTS

The halving or half-lap joint is a simple joint to cut and assemble, and involves removing half the thickness of each component at the joint position to form a neat-looking joint with the two components fitting flush with each other. Compared with the butt joint, it greatly strengthens corner, T and X joints in frameworks of all sorts since the interlocking shoulders of the joints help to resist twisting and also provide a greater contact area for gluing.

To make a corner halving joint (3), first ensure that the two ends to be joined are cut square. Then lay one component in position over the other and use a marking knife to mark the width of each piece across the face of the other component. Square this line all round each piece, then use a marking gauge to scribe a line to half the wood's thickness on each edge of both components.

Now cramp each component in turn in a vice and saw into the end-grain with a tenon saw, down to the marked line. Then lay each one flat on a bench hook and saw across the grain down to the first cut to remove the waste piece. Check that the two components fit well together, then apply waterproof woodworking adhesive to one component and assemble the joint, cramping it for maximum bond strength until the adhesive has set. Reinforce the joint with nails or screws.

For T and X (cross-halving) joints you need to cut a notch in one (T) or both (X) components. As before, use one piece to mark the position and width of the notch on the other component, then use the marking gauge again to scribe a line to half the wood's thickness. Saw down to this line on both sides of the notch to the scribed line, then use a sharp chisel to pare away the waste wood between the two saw cuts. Check that the notch has a flat base and cleanly-trimmed sides, then assemble the joint. The other component will have a halving-jointed end for a T-joint (4), or a matching notch for a cross-halving joint.

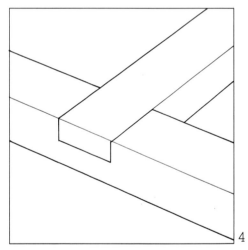

4

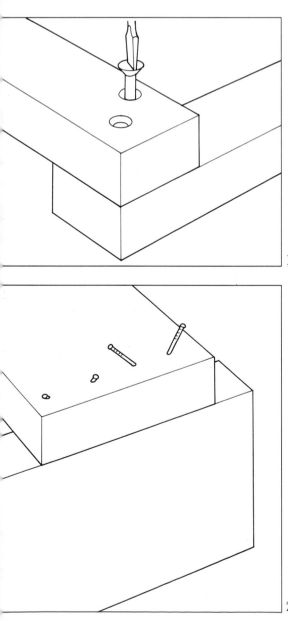

1

2

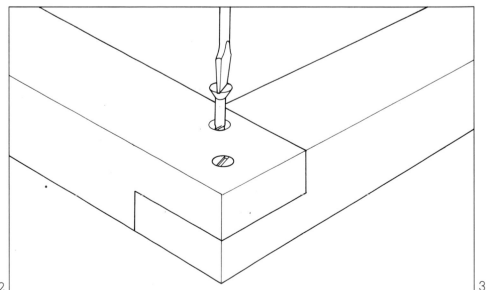

3

MORTISE-AND-TENON JOINT

This joint provides the strongest and neatest joint you are ever likely to require for your garden construction projects. It consists of a slot (the mortise) cut in one component into which a tongue (the tenon) cut on the other component fits. There are several variations, but the simplest is the through tenon, where a long tongue passes right through an open slot cut in the mortised component. The stopped version has a blind slot and a shorter tongue, giving a joint where no vulnerable end-grain is exposed to the elements.

To cut a mortise-and-tenon joint, start by preparing the piece with the tenon – component A (5). Lay the piece to be mortised – component B – across the end of A, to leave the tenon slightly over-long for later trimming. Square this shoulder line all round A, then select a chisel with a blade width as close as possible to one-third of the wood's thickness and set the two pins of a mortise gauge to match the blade width. Use the gauge to scribe the tenon width lines onto the edges and end of component A. Cramp it in a vice and saw down the scribed lines to the shoulder line, then set it on a bench hook so you can remove the two pieces of waste wood by sawing down the shoulder lines.

Next, lay A across B at the point where the mortise is to be cut, and mark the width of A on B. Square the lines all round B, then use the marking gauge with the pins set to the same separation as for marking the tenon to scribe the mortise width lines on the edges of B. Hold it edge up in a vice and drill out most of the waste from the mortise using either a spade bit in a power drill or an auger in a brace. Finally, use a chisel to remove the rest of the waste wood, working from both sides of the mortise to leave a neat, square-sided slot. Test the tenon for fit, and pare a little more wood from the sides of the mortise if it is too tight.

To assemble the joint, apply wood-working adhesive to the faces and shoulders of the tenon and insert it in the mortise (6). Check that the joint is square and cramp the two parts together if the structure allows and you have sash cramps long enough to span it. When the adhesive has set, plane off the end of the tenon so it is flush with the surrounding wood.

USING NAILS AND SCREWS

Most of the fixings you use for your garden projects will be nails or screws. Make sure that they are galvanized or otherwise rustproofed for outdoor use. As mentioned earlier, you should always fix the thinner component to the thicker one, using a fixing about three times longer than the thinner component. As far as diameter is concerned, the nail size selected will determine its thickness. For screws, the shank diameter should be no more than one-tenth the thickness of the wood it is being driven into.

When driving nails, ensure that the hammer head strikes the nail head squarely so you do not bend it; pull out

and replace any that do bend. Use a nail punch to drive the nail head fractionally below the wood surface.

When driving screws, remember that for all but the smallest screws you must drill two screw holes before you drive the screw in. You need a clearance hole in the thinner component to prevent the shank of the screw from jamming or splitting the wood, and a pilot hole in the thicker component to accept the threaded tip of the screw. If you want the screw head to lie flush with the wood surface, you also need a countersink – a conical recess formed in the wood with a countersinking bit. As a guide, the clearance hole should be the same diameter as the screw shank, while the pilot hole should be about two-thirds of the thread diameter and about 6mm ($1/4$in) less than the thread length.

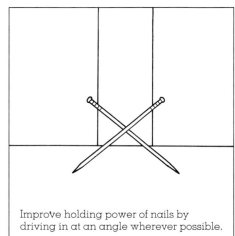

Improve holding power of nails by driving in at an angle wherever possible.

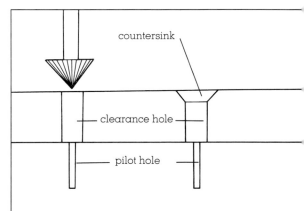

USING COACH BOLTS

You may prefer to use coach bolts and nuts to assemble heavy-duty structures. Simply drill a clearance hole through both components to match the bolt diameter, insert the bolt, add a washer and tighten the nut with a spanner. The action of tightening the nut will draw the squared-off section beneath the bolt head into the wood, preventing it turning and helping to lock the structure securely together.

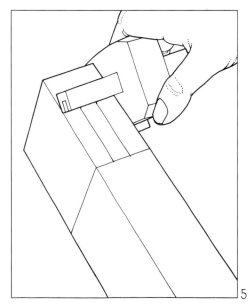

5

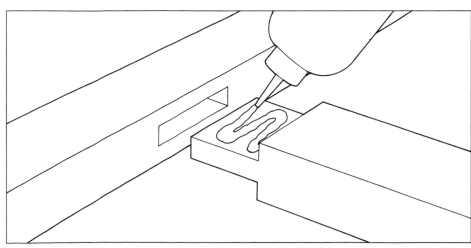

6

Techniques

Wood preservatives and finishes

The trouble with wood is that it is a natural material, and Mother Nature is always trying to reclaim her own – by attacking it relentlessly with sun, wind, rain, wood-boring insects and wood-eating fungi. Preservatives help to stem the attack.

The biggest enemy of wood is moisture, because it provides the perfect conditions for natural forces to thrive and eventually to destroy it. Outside the house, any exposed woodwork will be damp for long periods, and these are precisely the conditions which encourage rot and insect attack. Most at risk is any timber in direct contact with the ground.

Types of preservative

Perhaps the best known and, until recently, the most widely used wood preservative for outdoor use is creosote. This is formed from the distillation of coal tar, and is a dark or golden brown liquid easily applied to surfaces such as fences and sheds by brush or spray. Creosote's main drawbacks are that it soon weathers, so repeated applications are needed; it is unpleasant to handle – many people suffer skin irritation when using it – and is toxic to plants coming into contact with treated surfaces; it is also difficult to overpaint once applied. However, it is cheap.

Organic solvent preservatives were developed precisely to get round these drawbacks. They consist of fungicidal and insecticidal agents dissolved in an organic solvent – usually white spirit – which helps to ensure deep penetration of the wood. They can be applied by brush or spray, or for the best penetration, by immersing the wood in the liquid for a period of up to 24 hours. Once the solvent has evaporated, the wood can be painted or varnished if desired. Some types incorporate wood stains, which help to colour and enhance the look of the wood grain and make other finishes unnecessary. Others incorporate water-repellent additives to further improve the wood's resistance to moisture. They are generally less messy to apply than creosote, and any after-smell soon disappears as the solvent evaporates. However, they are highly inflammable, so must be used with care. Special horticultural grades are available which are non-toxic to plants.

Water-based preservatives have been around for many years, but are mainly used for the pre-treatment of structural timbers and the like by pressure impregnation. Recently-introduced water-based preservatives for DIY application are easier to apply than solvent-based ones, have little smell, are easy to wash from hands, clothes and brushes and are harmless to plants. Some types also incorporate stains and water-repellent additives. However, they do not penetrate wood to the same degree as the organic solvent types, and are therefore recommended for use on timbers not in direct contact with the ground.

Microporous finishes

One of the problems of keeping rot and woodworm at bay lies in the use of traditional paint or varnish systems on much exterior woodwork. These trap moisture beneath the film surface, encouraging rot to spread especially if the wood itself was not preservative-treated.

One solution to this problem is to use so-called microporous or 'breathing' products instead. These form a waterproof coating to the wood, but allow moisture vapour to evaporate through them without causing the tell-tale blisters and cracks that plague traditional finishes. The end result is a finish that stays effective and good-looking for longer, and is also easier to maintain in the future than gloss paint or varnish coatings.

Microporous finishes are available in opaque or translucent form – in other words as 'paint' or 'varnish'; which you choose will depend on whether you want a coloured finish or one that enhances the natural look of the wood grain. Microporous paints are available in a wide range of colours, and have a gloss or semi-gloss finish. Microporous stains come chiefly in natural wood shades – teak, oak, mahogany, cedar and so on – and come in matt and semi-gloss finishes.

To perform as they are intended to, microporous products have to be applied to bare wood – usually as a two coat system. This means that existing

Above: *This attractive summer house will soon need attention. Check wooden structures annually for damage.*

paint or varnish films have to be stripped off completely first. They do not themselves have any preservative action (although the translucent stains incorporate ultra-violet filters to help reduce degradation of the wood fibres by sunlight). It is therefore still important that wood being treated with these products has adequate preservative protection. This means either applying one of the wood preservatives mentioned earlier, or ensuring that all bought wood has been pre-treated by the supplier.

Repairing fences

The fences round your property deserve to be as well looked after as any other part of the house and garden. If they are, they will look good, help keep intruders (human and animal) out and define your property boundaries clearly in case of territorial disputes with your neighbours. If they are not, they are just an inefficient eyesore that will be a constant source of irritation to all parties.

Checking ownership

Before you even contemplate any work on your fences, make sure you know which ones are your responsibility and which are your neighbours' preserve. There are no hard and fast rules about this: your deeds may state who owns which fence, and there is a common assumption that the fence is yours if the supporting posts are on your side. Also, with board-and-rail fences it is sensible to assume that the boards were fixed to the rails from the owner's side. Some fences are legally designated as 'party fences', which means both owners must share maintenance costs. If ownership is unclear, try to reach a sensible agreement with your neighbours; ideally this should be in writing so that disputes are avoided in future years.

Making an inspection

Checking your fences is a perfect weekend job. Walk round your boundaries and inspect the condition of posts, intermediate boards, rails and panels, and check that fixings are sound and posts are secure. If everything is in good condition, some simple cosmetic and preservative treatment may be all that is needed, but if you have neglected your fences you may be in for some more substantial repair work.

Using preservatives

If you have wooden fences that are in good condition, it will pay you to keep them that way by treating the wood with preservative to keep rot and insect attack at bay. See Types of preservative for more details. It is a simple matter to apply any of these treatments to your fences, although if you have plants growing up the fence or nearby you should either use a type harmless to plants or pull them away from the fence carefully and protect them with polythene. Use an old brush or a garden spray gun, and pay particular attention to end grain and to sections close to ground level.

Structural repairs

If you find that your fence is not in particularly good health, it is better to repair it now than to have to replace it completely in another few years.

If you have a close-boarded fence, remove rotten boards by punching their fixing nails through into the rails behind, then slide in a new length of feather-edged board which has been liberally treated with preservative. Use a spacer to gauge the correct overlap between boards, and nail the new board in place to the rails.

Repair breaks or splits in the rails by nailing on proprietary galvanised metal repair brackets – the straight type for breaks in the centre of the rail, the flared-end type for repairs to the ends of the rails where the tenon may have rotted away or pulled out of its mortise.

Remove rotten gravel boards and their fixing blocks, treat the bottom ends of the fence boards with preservative and nail a new gravel board to new blocks (again well treated with preservative).

If you have a panel fence, check that the fixing nails have not caused splits in the sides of the panel, and drive in fresh galvanised nails if the panel is loose. Replace panels that are badly split or warped; you can cut panels down to size by removing the vertical battens, sawing down the panel and replacing the battens.

Repairs to fence posts

If you find that a fence post has worked loose, dig out the soil round the base of the post to see if it has rotted away. If it seems sound, brush on a liberal dose of preservative; then ram some bricks in firmly round the bottom of the post and anchor it with a collar of concrete about 150mm (6in) thick.

If the underground section of the post has rotted away completely, you can either fit a completely new fence post or else save the sound part and use a concrete fence spur or fence spike to secure it.

With a concrete spur, you avoid having to dismantle part of the fence run. First, saw through the post just above ground level and remove the rotten part. Then dig a hole beneath the post, and set the spur in the hole. Check that it is vertical, then mark the post through the bolt holes in the spur, drill the fixing holes through the post, and brush preservative into the holes. Finally, bolt the post to the spur using galvanised nuts, bolts and washers, ram in hardcore round the base of the spur,

and top it off with a collar of concrete, sloped at the top so rainwater runs away from the post.

With a fence spike, you have to remove the old post first. Cut through the arris rails next to the posts, or prise out any panel fixing nails, ease the adjoining fence sections away from the post, and provide temporary support for them. Lever out the post using stout timber roped to the post as a lever and some bricks to act as a fulcrum, and saw off the rotten part. Compact the ground thoroughly where the old post was removed, then hammer in the fence spike and check that it is vertical. Set the post in the top of the spike, and screw or bolt it in place. Finally, replace panels, either with nails or using small C-shaped metal brackets; with close-boarded types, re-attach the arris rails with metal repair brackets.

Lastly, make sure that the vulnerable tops of the fence posts are protected from moisture penetration by nailing on a shaped wooden capping piece.

Other structures

Other wooden garden structures also need looking after if they are to remain in good condition, yet many are sadly neglected. Replacements are not cheap any more. so it pays to put right defects before they get serious, and to include such structures in your annual property maintenance round.

If rot has begun to attack but has not yet seriously affected the timber, treat it as a matter of urgency with two or three generous coats of preservative (see above). Before applying this, scrub down the timber surfaces thoroughly to remove surface dirt and growths of lichen or algae. Then brush on the first coat, working from the bottom up to avoid drip marks, and apply a second when the first has dried. Most preservatives are rather splashy to use, so lay polythene sheeting round the structure to protect paving, lawn or plants.

If rot damage has already occurred on a small scale, you may be able to patch it using a wood repair kit. This consists of a hardener to consolidate and strengthen damaged wood, plus a filler to make good missing parts. However, these kits are designed for making repairs that will be overpainted, and the patches will be rather noticeable on a typical timber outbuilding with a natural finish. A better solution is to cut out the rotten timber carefully and to replace it with new, preservative treated wood. You will have to take this course anyway if the damage is widespread.

Left: *Wear gloves when applying creosote as it can irritate the skin.*

GLOSSARY

Baulk of timber – large section of Lumber
Bricklaying sand – Masonry Sand
Budgerigars – Parakeets
Builders Merchant – Builders Supplier
Chestnut Paling – Snow Fence – Split Pole Fence
Chop Saw – Bench-top Mitre Saw – Cut off Saw
Chipboard – Particle Board
Circular Saw – Skil Saw
Clout Nails – Roofing Nails
Coach Bolts – Carriage Bolts
Crazy Paving – Irregular Stone
DPC – Damp Proof Course
Hardcore – Coarse or broken aggregate, such as brick or stone
Interference or Interlap Fencing – Alternate Board – Board & Board
J-Bolt – Anchor Bolt
MDF/Medium Density Fibreboard – MDO/Medium Density Overlay – Chipboard
Micro-porous Paint – Latex Stain
Nail Punch – Nail Set
Planed Timber – Dimensional Lumber – PAR Timber
Planning Permission – Zoning Approval
Plant Hire Firm – Equipment Rental Company
Railway Sleepers – Railroad Ties
Re-decorate – Re-paint externally
Ridged Roof – Pitched Roof
Services – Utilities
Silver Sand – Sharp Sand – River Sand
Skew-nail – Toe-nail
Flat Bit – Space Bit
Spanner – Wrench
Spirit level – Level
Tamp Down – Compact
Timber – Lumber
Timber Cladding – Clapboarding
Timber Merchant – Lumber Yard
Try Square – Carpenter's Square
Turf – Sod
Waney-edged Board – Rough Sawn Plank
Willow Hurdle – Woven Sapling Fencing

CHOOSING WOOD

For most of the projects featured in this book you will probably be using the most economical timber available in your area. This is likely to be a softwood, such as redwood, pressure treated southern yellow pine or cedar (US); redwood, pine, larch, spruce or red cedar (UK); South African pine, jelutong or honey wood (RSA); radiata pine, Oregon red cedar (Australia). Some species, such as white cedar, are naturally resistant to rot and insect attack, but others, such as southern yellow pine, need pressure preservative treatment for outdoor use.

If you want to use a hardwood – to make garden furniture perhaps – you are likely to have a different range of choices that will include both temperate species, such as oak (US), ash and elm (UK) and tropical hardwoods such as teak, iroko* and ramin* (*except the US). Eucalyptus is widely used for fence poles in the RSA while in the US white cedar or pressure treated pine would be the best choice of timber for this purpose.

INDEX